UNIQUE MEETING PLACES IN GREATER WASHINGTON

UNIQUE MEETING PLACES IN GREATER WASHINGTON

Distinctive Conference
and Party Facilities Found Only
in the Capital Area

ELISE FORD

EPM

Library of Congress Cataloging-in-Publication Data

Ford, Elise.
    Unique meeting places in Greater Washington: distinctive
    party and conference facilities found only in the capital area /
    Elise Ford with the Washington Association Research
    Foundation.
        p.   cm.
    Includes index.
    ISBN 0-939009-08-0
    1. Convention facilities—Washington Metropolitan Area—
Guide-books.   I. Washington Association Research Foundation.
II. Title. TX907.F583 1988
647'.94753—dc19   88-3566
                                                                        CIP

Copyright © 1988 Elise Ford with the Washington Association
    Research Foundation
All Rights Reserved
EPM Publications, Inc., 1003 Turkey Run Road
    McLean, VA 22101
Printed in the United States of America

Cover and book design by Tom Huestis
Original drawings by Pauline Lange: Arts Club of Washington
    (cover), C&O *Canal Clipper*, Carlyle House, Fondo del Sol,
    Newton White Mansion Conservatory, Calvert Collection,
    Decatur Carriage House, Meridian House International,
    Woodrow Wilson House, Corcoran Gallery of Art, Oxon Hill
    Manor Garden Gate, Woodlawn Manor House Gazebo

Contents

5

SITES FOR 200 TO 500 PEOPLE

SITES FOR 500 TO 1,000 PEOPLE

SITES FOR MORE THAN 1,000 PEOPLE

*This breakdown identifies the maximum number of people a site can accommodate for any type of event. Refer to the individual site descriptions to determine specific capacity information for a particular type of event.

Foreword

By day, the Phillips Collection, in the Dupont Circle area of Washington, D.C., is a magnificent art museum that attracts visitors from all over the world. At night, this former private mansion is often the scene of some of the city's most elegant receptions.

By day, exotic fish and sea creatures swim and play in the waters of the National Aquarium, while delighted school children and adults look on in wonder. By night, gala banquets, as colorful as the inhabitants of the illuminated tanks, make this, the oldest aquarium in the country, one of the most exciting party places in the nation's capital.

In fact, day or night, Washington's museums, federal buildings, and historic homes frequently are the settings of meetings and social events hosted by associations, corporations, other organizations and individuals who want their gatherings to be unforgettable.

For example, an association's Board of Directors meets in a gracious Georgian-style townhouse near Embassy Row that also happens to be the former home of the 28th president of the United States. Corporate VIPs sit down to dinner at the Arts Club of Washington, the 1802 mansion where James Monroe once lived; and even the most sophisticated party-goer is thrilled by an invitation to the Calvert Collection, a splendid museum filled with paintings, sculpture, and antique furniture. While these and many more unique and impressive meeting and party sites exist in and around the city of Washington, until now there has been no single source of information about them. That is why the Washington Association Research Foundation—the research and scholarship arm of the Greater Washington Society of Association Executives—made the research grant for this book.

Designed as a tool for use by association and corporate meeting planners, *Unique Meeting Places in Greater Washington* also will be of interest to area residents who are making arrangements for weddings or other private functions. Though most people know that the Washington area has a profusion of outstanding hotels and restaurants and that its convention center is one of the best in the country, many may not realize that the area abounds with intriguing places that one may rent for a special occasion. This book fills that void.

The Washington Association Research Foundation was established in 1982 by the Greater Washington Society of Association Executives to conduct research into subjects of importance and concern to the association community in the greater Washington area and to share its findings with members of that community and all others who are interested. The Foundation is delighted, therefore, that this book will not only reach meeting planners and residents in the national capital area, but also will be available to a broad spectrum of associations and organizations in the United States and elsewhere.

The Foundation wishes to thank the following sponsors for their support of this project and for their foresight in helping to make the book possible:

Capital Informer, Inc.
The Hilton Hotels of Greater Washington
The Hyatt Hotels of Greater Washington
The Sheraton Hotels of Greater Washington
Washington D.C. Convention and Visitors Association
WashingtonInc.

A special salute goes to Ilsa Whittemore, Associate Executive Director, Hotel Sales and Marketing Association International. It was she, as Chairman of the Foundation's Projects Survey and Research Committee, who suggested the idea for the book and helped to initiate its research, writing and publication.

Finally, we want to thank Michelle Ferrier, Wendy Mann and Karen Schumacher of the Foundation's professional staff, for their dedicated help in creating this valuable guide to the *Unique Meeting Places in Greater Washington*.

STEPHEN W. CAREY, CAE, Ph.D.

Executive Director
Washington Association Research Foundation

Washington, D.C.
March 1988

How to Use This Book

It's no secret that Washington, D.C., is brimming with wonderfully unique meeting places. People have been holding business conferences and social events here for years—hundreds of years. Think about it: When George Washington wanted to gather with his forefather friends in a relaxed setting, where did he go? (Gadsby's Tavern in Old Town Alexandria was one favorite spot.) When Washington's stepson, John Parke Custis, married Eleanor Calvert—the Calvert family founded Maryland—in 1774, where do you think they held the wedding? (Mount Airy Plantation, the bride's home in Upper Marlboro, Maryland.) And where did President Madison sign the Treaty of Ghent ending the War of 1812, since the White House had been torched by the British? (At the nearby Octagon, where James and Dolley holed up after the siege.)

Or consider the events of more modern times: Just where are all those inaugural balls held, anyway? (The Pavilion at the Old Post Office and the National Building Museum, to name two.) What kind of lavish accommodations did the Iranians use for their legendary parties before they were kicked out of the country? (An Iranian mansion on Embassy Row that now houses an annex of the State Department.) Where do Sylvester Stallone and his Potomac Polo Club teammates celebrate after playing polo on the mall? (The U.S. Department of Agriculture Patio.)

All of these places, and many more, are available to you and are included in *Unique Meeting Places*.

If you know exactly where you want to stage your Washington event, simply flip to the Alphabetic Index and find the page number for the site description. Each of the guide's nearly 100 entries provides facts about capacity, location, food and beverage arrangements, rates, limitations and restrictions, lead time for reserving, and facilities for the physically handicapped.

But maybe you haven't made up your mind about a site, or else you're ready for some new ideas. Or maybe your ideal setting doesn't meet the specific requirements of your group. If you're just starting to plan your function, you may not yet know what your group's requirements are. Perhaps you have a vague idea of what you want but aren't sure what's available in the area.

So how do you uncover the unique Washington site that's guaranteed to suit your group and its event to a T?

This guide will help. In addition to its ultimate purpose of assisting you in finding the perfect setting for your function, the book may be used, first, as a tool in the meeting-planning process to help you arrive at answers to basic questions, the same questions you can expect to be asked by the staff at each site. These questions are:

- *When is the event taking place?*

- *How many people will be attending?*

- *What type of event will it be?*

- *Do you want it indoors, outdoors or both?*

- *What is your budget?*

- *What are your special requirements? For example, do you have specific music, food or drink, or equipment requirements?*

The guide is organized by capacity categories since the one piece of information that meeting planners often know from the start is the general number of people expected to attend the function. Please note: The sites included in each section are those whose *maximum* capacities fall into a particular category. Maximum capacities reflect the total space available, usually including the grounds. If you wish to know how many people can be accommodated indoors alone or within one portion of the site, or for a particular type of event, you should refer to the specific information provided for each site.

Once you've determined the specific sites that can accommodate your group, it's up to you to choose the place you want. A Topical Cross Reference at the back of the book identifies sites by special interest. If you're interested in throwing a large outdoor picnic, look under the "Picnic Site" heading for J.R.'s Festival Lakes located outside Leesburg in Virginia, or Smokey Glen Farm in Gaithersburg, Maryland. If you're holding an overnight event, go down the list of the overnight conference centers. Do you want your event to be imbued with a sense of history? You've got 46 choices, all found under the "Historical Sites" heading in the cross reference index.

Perhaps you're not keen on traveling far from your office or hotel; in such case, you should refer to the Geographic Index for sites located near your group's central quarters.

Certainly the budget factor will figure in your choice of a site. Specific rates are provided in each site description, so simply consult there to decide whether your budget covers the stated costs. The rates quoted herein are those provided by the sites at the time the book was researched in late 1987.

In addition to rental costs, there are usually other expenses, some of which can be quite substantial. Take catering, for instance. A three-hour cocktail reception for 50 people is likely to run you at least $1,500; adding dinner will double that; and if you really want to go down in history, some caterers will gladly help you spend as much as $250 per person. Tent rental is another major expense. Prices start at about $300 for a small tent and go as high as the tens of thousands for the largest size tent equipped with special, but sometimes necessary, items such as lighting, guttering, a dance floor and heaters.

There are other things you should know as you read this book. The word "reception" used throughout refers to any stand-up event; the word "banquet" refers to any type of sit-down function. The serving of alcohol is permitted at most sites; therefore, the book notes only exceptions or restrictions on the use thereof. For example, Collingwood-on-the-Potomac allows only beer, wine and champagne to be served; the Corcoran Gallery of Art, like many sites, prohibits red wine because it can stain.

Regulations and procedures for serving alcoholic beverages vary from jurisdiction to jurisdiction. Chances are, however, that you won't have to obtain a special liquor permit since most meeting places are already fully licensed or else handle the permit process for you. Fairfax County Park Authority sites in Virginia are one exception. At Colvin Run Mill, Green Spring Farm and other Park Authority facilities, you're required to complete an application and pay $30 (if you're a Fairfax County resident) or $60 (if you're not a county resident) for an alcoholic beverage use permit.

13

Staff at each site will provide you with exact information regarding jurisdictional requirements for serving alcohol.

Most meeting places ask you to adhere to certain rules when you rent their facilities. One site may prohibit smoking, for example, and another not allow fundraising. The book lists these rules of usage along with site limitations under the heading "Limitations/Restrictions" included in each description. The list is not necessarily all-inclusive for each site but is intended to give you an idea of the most important use considerations.

You'll notice the recurring phrase "Call for availability" when you come to the "Lead Time for Reservations" portion of each site description. While many places are fairly specific about their reservation schedules, others find their schedules less predictable. These facilities prefer you to go ahead and give them a call, no matter the lead time, on the chance that a cancellation or other unexpected circumstance makes their site available when you need it.

The question "Facilities for the Physically Handicapped?" appears at the end of each entry. A check mark under "Yes" indicates that the site itself and a restroom are accessible to someone in a wheelchair. A check mark under "No" means that neither the site nor its restrooms is accessible to someone in a wheelchair. A "Some" notation followed by a brief explanation lets you know that the site is partially accessible to someone in a wheelchair and just what those accessible facilities are.

Finally, two special sections at the end of the book tell you how to book group seats at Washington's theaters, arrange briefings on Capitol Hill with congressional members or at the White House with administration officials, and schedule private tours of the White House.

So there you have it, 93 meeting places that range from capacious to cozy, quaint to sophisticated, simple to elaborate, and all unique. Whatever your dream setting, Washington offers a lot to choose from.

Sites for Fewer than 50 People

BELMONT CONFERENCE CENTER

6555 Belmont Woods Road
Elkridge, Maryland 21227
301/796-4300

An elegant, age-old business retreat

Lots of historic homes offer elegant meeting facilities. After a certain hour, however, most places require you to head on home or back to your hotel, whether or not you're truly finished with business. Not so at Belmont.

When you confer at Belmont, you reside here. Although the term "conference center" has a modern ring to it, Belmont is actually an early 18th-century mansion that sits secluded on 365 acres of rolling fields and woods leading down to the Patapsco River. Inside the cream-colored stucco building are 15 bedrooms that can accommodate 25 guests; a conference room (complete with audiovisual and other equipment) and a dining room, each of which seats 35; and a drawing room, library, tea room and ballroom for social gatherings.

Belmont looks and feels like a gracious country inn, only there are no other guests when your group stays here. Each room is charmingly decorated in attractive colonial colors and 18th-century-style furnishings. Especially lovely are the drawing room, whose overstuffed, floral-patterned sofa and chairs invite you to sink into them, and the ballroom, a mix of mauve, blue and rose colors, antique furniture and a working fireplace.

Belmont offers you ways to break from business without leaving the grounds. There are formal gardens, paths through woods and fields for walking or jogging, tennis courts and a swimming pool. For the ornithologists among you, at least 117 species of birds have been sighted here.

CAPACITY

Reception: 35
Banquet: 35
Garden party: 100 to 150
Meeting: 35
Accommodations: 25
Belmont can arrange for additional, nearby sleeping accommodations when the number of your party exceeds 25.

LOCATION

From Washington: Go north on U.S. I-95 to the Route 100 exit (marked Glen Burnie); go right at the exit and travel until you get to Route 1; go left on Route 1, then left on Montgomery Road, then right on Elibank Drive to Belmont Woods Road; turn left on Belmont Woods Road to Belmont.

FOOD/BEVERAGE

Belmont caters all conference meals and works with the group to plan the menus.

LIMITATIONS/RESTRICTIONS

No specific limitations; discuss your requests with management.

LEAD TIME FOR RESERVATIONS

At least eight weeks, but Belmont will accept reservations two years in advance.

RATES

$115 per person per day. This rate covers overnight accommodations, three meals, two coffee breaks and exclusive use of the house. There are no service charges. The rates and rate structure are expected to change in 1988.

FACILITIES FOR THE PHYSICALLY HANDICAPPED?
YES NO SOME
      X

C & O CANAL BOATS

The Georgetown: 1055 Thomas Jefferson Street, N.W.
Washington, D.C. 20007
202-472-4376
Canal Clipper: 11710 MacArthur Boulevard
Potomac, Maryland 20854
301/299-2026

A moving experience of the past

Once you set foot on one of these boats you have no choice
but to sit back, relax, enjoy the scenery and take in some
history.

The C & O Canal is 184½ miles long, stretching from Cum-
berland, Maryland, to Georgetown in Washington, D.C.;
but you travel only a small portion of that distance. As you
rest on wooden benches that line the sides of these long,
flat-roofed pine boats, costumed park rangers regale you
with stories about life along the canal in the 1870s, when
the waterway was in its heyday. You can watch as the rangers hitch up the mules that will lead the boat up the canal
along the tow path, and you'll see them work the boat
through the lock just as was done decades ago.

Two boats are in service, and each uses a different seg-
ment of the restored canal. If you board the *Canal Clipper*
in Great Falls Park, Maryland, you'll travel past beautiful
dense woods and see geese and ducks and probably the
occasional jogger or bike rider. *The Georgetown* takes you
through the old canal district, past both historic townhouses
and chic shops.

CAPACITY

Boat party: 60

LOCATION

You board The Georgetown *on the canal between 30th and
Thomas Jefferson Streets, N.W., in Georgetown. Foggy Bottom*

19

is the closest Metro station. To board the Canal Clipper, you can take Beltway exit 41W to Great Falls Park, which lies at the end of MacArthur Boulevard in Potomac, Maryland.

FOOD/BEVERAGE

You make your own food and drink arrangements.

LIMITATIONS/RESTRICTIONS

Smoking and alcohol are prohibited. The boats operate from mid-April through mid-October. You should call for information about hours and days of operation.

LEAD TIME FOR RESERVATIONS

Make reservations as far in advance as possible, starting in March of each year.

RATES

$450 for a two-hour trip.

FACILITIES FOR THE PHYSICALLY HANDICAPPED?
YES NO SOME
     X

The barges are accessible to individuals in wheelchairs.

HAPPY DAZE VI

600 Water Street, S.W.

NBU-7-11

Washington, D.C. 20024

202/554-5047

For yachting parties on the Potomac

Every business and association should have its own *Happy Daze VI* yacht. Just think how nice it would be to have: a special place to entertain clients; intimate, extra-secluded meeting quarters where you can brainstorm for fresh ideas, drawing inspiration from the soothing ride along the river; a luxurious cruise vessel for throwing parties to reward yourselves for work well done.

If you don't have a yacht of your own, the next best thing, of course, is to rent *Happy Daze*. Measuring 65 feet in length, with three decks, *Happy Daze* is a lot of yacht. Starting with the lowest deck, you can hole up in the hull and hold a meeting in the cozy sitting room. The middle deck is enclosed and can be used for any purpose. This one-room area is very stylishly furnished with brown leather chairs and sofa, Honduras mahogany paneled walls, brass light fixtures and miniblinds on the many windows. There are also a piano and a "one-armed bandit" (i.e., a slot machine), both of which you are welcome to play.

The top deck is high and open, granting you a great view of Washington's sights. You can settle back against the white-cushioned seats, listen to the music wafting on the wind from the bi-level stereo and enjoy cocktails and conversation with your colleagues. This deck holds a bar at one end.

Dockside events are possible, as well.

CAPACITY

Reception: 49
Banquet: 49
Meeting: 49

LOCATION

The yacht is docked on the Washington waterfront in southwest Washington; however, you board her at one of two locations: Georgetown Harbor or the Alexandria Marina.

FOOD/BEVERAGE

You're free to choose your own caterer or the one recommended by the yacht's owner. Happy Daze *stocks a premium bar.*

LIMITATIONS/RESTRICTIONS

Cigarette smoking is allowed but not cigars or pipes. Dancing is not allowed.

LEAD TIME FOR RESERVATIONS

Call for availability.

RATES

$1,400 for three hours, plus $250 for each additional hour. This rate covers the fee for the full crew, including the bartender. In addition, there is a $15 per person charge for an open bar serving premium brands and setups.

FACILITIES FOR THE PHYSICALLY HANDICAPPED?
YES NO SOME
   X

THE LAFAYETTE

1020 16th Street, N.W.
Washington, D.C. 20036
202/223-8788

Elite accommodations at a downtown address

A green awning outside its entrance calls your attention to the Lafayette; otherwise you might not notice this quietly distinguished, Federal-Baroque-style brick townhouse. Once you do notice it, though, you'll probably agree that the place exudes an air of good taste, exclusivity and utter privacy.

Inside, it's the same. The Lafayette has all the look and feel of an elite club. In fact, the building once housed the Gaslight Club, a sort of rich man's city retreat, from the 1950s to the 1980s. Before that, this was the home of Ulysses S. Grant III, the president's grandson. In 1984, the Wynmark Development Corporation purchased the building and converted it into luxury residential and office suites on the top floors, a conference room and reception area on the lobby level, and a banquet room on the lower level.

The conference room, reception area and banquet room are the primary rental areas, but you may also use the roof-top terrace or even one of the luxury suites, if one is available. Petite sitting rooms on either side of the inside entrance and an extended hall comprise the reception area, which is set off by mahogany inlaid oak floors, oak panelling and a white damask Chippendale sofa.

Walk across the Italian marble floor to the back of the townhouse and you arrive at the richly appointed conference room. Here you can sink into one of the twelve commodious brown leather chairs that surround the long and heavy wood table. Grasscloth wall coverings, recessed lights and color-coordinated carpeting and curtains are some of the more decorative flourishes.

Downstairs, the banquet room awaits you. (A computerized voice in the elevator lets you know that you are descending.) A bright, multicolored rug, Queen Anne chairs and full-length swagged draperies are some of the features of this chamber.

If you want the feel of a private and exquisitely furnished apartment, but have no reason or prefer not to hold the event at someone's home or at a hotel, consider reserving one of the Lafayette's luxury suites. Each suite has been decorated by a different interior designer and features lavish accommodations including woodburning fireplaces and marble floors.

To give a "midnight in Manhattan" feel to your event, you can convene on the roof. Atop the building's eighth floor is an outdoor terrace that overlooks downtown Washington, a sight most impressive at night when the city sounds ebb and city lights give you an uncommon view of the capital.

CAPACITY

Reception: from 6 to 50
Banquet: from 6 to 50
Conferences: from 6 to 50

LOCATION

Three blocks from the White House, directly across from the Capitol Hilton hotel.

FOOD/BEVERAGE

The Lafayette normally handles all the catering arrangements but will allow you to choose your own caterer, if you prefer.

LIMITATIONS/RESTRICTIONS

The Lafayette has no specific restrictions, but you should review your requests with management.

LEAD TIME FOR RESERVATIONS

Call for availability.

RATES

A flat rate of $250 for an all-day conference in either the conference room or the banquet room. For all other events, there is no room rental charge—you pay only the catering fee, which usually averages about $25 to $30 a person for a sit-down dinner, not including drinks.

FACILITIES FOR THE PHYSICALLY HANDICAPPED?
YES NO SOME
X

OLD TOWN TROLLEY TOURS OF WASHINGTON

3150 V Street, N.E.
Washington, D.C. 20018
202/269-3020

Set your meeting in motion

You may not accomplish much business aboard the Old Town Trolleys, but that's the point. These stylized trolleys don't run on a track; they're set on a truck chassis. Painted green and orange, and modeled after trolleys that ran in the early 1900s, the vehicles wind their way around Washington allowing you a chance to unwind, socialize and sightsee, all at the same time. Even if you're a native Washingtonian, you may learn a thing or two about the capital from the narrated tour.

The trolleys travel in all weather. The interior of each car is furnished with brass fixtures and comfortable, green-cushioned seats. You can choose the standard 15-stop route, which travels to the National Cathedral, Georgetown and Capitol Hill, among other places. Or you can charter one or more trolleys for a customized tour of the area, to Mount Vernon, for example, or to Old Town Alexandria. Either way, you can pretty much call your own shots. If you want to decorate the interior, play music, be entertained, and enjoy refreshments—it's all possible.

CAPACITY

Reception: 42 per trolley. There are ten trolleys.

LOCATION

Stay where you are! Old Town Trolley will come to you if you're located in the greater Washington area.

FOOD/BEVERAGE

The charter consultant can arrange for refreshments or you may do it yourself.

LIMITATIONS/RESTRICTIONS

Smoking and alcohol prohibited. The trolleys are not air-conditioned.

LEAD TIME FOR RESERVATIONS

Preferably six months in advance for charters. October through December is the busiest season.

RATES

$207 per trolley for the first two hours, plus $92 per trolley for each aditional hour.

FACILITIES FOR THE PHYSICALLY HANDICAPPED?
YES NO SOME
   X

Sites for
50 to 200 People

ADELPHI MILL

8402 Riggs Road
Adelphi, Maryland 20783
Mailing address: 6600 Kenilworth Avenue
Riverdale, Maryland 20737
301/699-2415

A bit of country in suburban Maryland

Set foot inside the Adelphi Mill and watch as a "country" spirit takes over your gathering. First thing, the pace slows; people amble over to greet each other rather than stride. Then a twang starts seeping into the conversations of even the most citified folks; and the next thing you know, a voice is heard urging everyone to swing his partner and do-si-do.

Adelphi Mill is available for a variety of functions, from business meetings to weddings, and any function you hold here will have an informal but fun air about it. Built around 1796, the mill is a three-story, thick-walled stone building with panelled ceilings, rough-hewn wood pillars, exposed beams and bare hardwood floors. In a word, rustic.

Each floor of the mill is one large open area. You enter the mill on the middle level, which offers a kitchen, a small alcove that might be used to set up a buffet table or country band, and a display of original mill equipment. Deep-set windows and hanging lamps provide the lighting throughout the mill. The bottom floor is rather dark and club-base-ment-like, and here you'll find a second kitchen as well as more of the old mill apparatus. The top floor is perhaps the cheeriest since it lets in the most light.

If you need more space or just a break from square dancing, you can mosey out to the stone courtyard in front of the mill or to the park that lies beyond. Or if you're moved by the historic significance of the mill (Adelphi is the oldest and largest mill in the Washington, D.C. area), go on across the road and take a look at the 200-year-old miller's cottage that still stands.

CAPACITY

Reception: 150
Banquet: 150
Meeting: 150

LOCATION

Close to the University of Maryland, about 45 minutes from downtown Washington. From the Beltway: Take Exit 28, New Hampshire Avenue, south; follow New Hampshire Avenue to left on Adelphi Road, then right on Riggs Road (Route 212) and right again onto the park grounds.

FOOD/BEVERAGE

You make your own food and beverage arrangements. The mill has two kitchens.

LIMITATIONS/RESTRICTIONS

The individual renting the mill must be a resident of either Montgomery or Prince George's County, Maryland. You may not use the mill for sales or fundraising activities. Parking is limited to 50 cars. Events must end by 11:45 P.M.

LEAD TIME FOR RESERVATIONS

Adelphi Mill is a popular spot because of its reasonable rates and roominess. The staff starts taking calls in August to reserve the mill for the coming year and recommends that you call in August or shortly thereafter.

RATES

Weekdays: $60 for a six-hour period, plus $10 for each additional hour. Friday through Sunday: $175 for a six-hour period, plus $25 for each additional hour.
A $55 refundable deposit confirms your reservation.

FACILITIES FOR THE PHYSICALLY HANDICAPPED?
YES NO SOME
X

AMERICAN SOCIETY OF ASSOCIATION EXECUTIVES (ASAE)

Conference Center
1575 Eye Street, N.W.
Washington, D.C. 20005
202/626-2799

Confer, then confabulate

You might think something called a conference center would be a place to do business only. But you'd be wrong. Tucked inside the ASAE building in the heart of Washington, D.C., is a sort of gathering ground for the conference-bound. One minute you're discussing business, the next you're convening for cocktails, all without leaving the room in this comfortable but professional meeting facility.

Two rooms make up the center: a theater with tiered seats and a board room. Each room supplies all the technological tools you need to conduct business in the most sophisticated fashion, from audiovisual equipment to telemarketing facilities to videotape machines. The tone set by the center's furnishings makes getting down to business a relaxing proposition. The forest green and mauve color scheme, high-backed chairs and swivel seats may soothe even the most frenetic conferees.

When you're ready for that break, voilà! You simply pull back the middle divider to join the theater and board room. If you're ready for an even bigger break, just step outside. The ASAE building is only minutes away from the White House, museums, restaurants and other city sights.

CAPACITY

Reception: 150
Banquet: 75

LOCATION

Three blocks from the White House, across the street from the McPherson Square Metro station.

FOOD/BEVERAGE

ASAE handles all rentals and catering. A small kitchen next to the board room is equipped with a microwave oven, refrigerator and stove.

LIMITATIONS/RESTRICTIONS

No specific limitations; discuss your requests with management.

LEAD TIME FOR RESERVATIONS

Three weeks to one month, but call for availability.

RATES

$270 to $425, depending on whether you're a member of ASAE and the length of time you're renting the conference center.

FACILITIES FOR THE PHYSICALLY HANDICAPPED?
YES NO SOME
X

AMERICAN ZEPHYR RAILROAD

815 15th Street, N.W., Suite 910
Washington, D.C. 20005
202/737-0818

Relaxing on the railroad

One way or another you can bet you're going places when you book your function on the American Zephyr Railroad.

The Railroad is actually two full-size rail cars that can either stay put for in-station festivities or hook up with an Amtrak train for movable fetes. When they were manufactured in the 1940s, the Zephyr trains represented a breakthrough in railroad technology. In recognition of their grand streamlined design, the cars were named for Zephyrus, the god of the west wind in Greek mythology. The American Zephyr corporation purchased the cars in 1983 and reconditioned them to make them compatible with Amtrak's fleet.

A lounge car and a dining car don't look much different from others on the track, but hop on board and you're in for a surprise. An art deco designer had a hand in the decor here. You can settle back in comfortable club chairs or on deep-set banquettes that hug the sides of the cars. There are oval-shaped chrome tables on which to place your drinks and when it's time for another round, just belly up to the burled walnut bar. Train cars are cozy places anyway, but the American Zephyr is especially so with its warm color scheme of cinnamon and deep purple.

A banquet aboard the Zephyr is like a trip back in time. You sit at tables covered with white linen tablecloths and set with art deco silver and Staffordshire china. Care for some barbecued steak? Yes, the full kitchen even features a charcoal grill.

It may never have occurred to you to hold a meeting on a train, but where else will you have so captive an audience? In addition to meetings, receptions and banquets, you can rent the railroad for pre- and post-conference travel and for the popular murder mystery trips. The cars are available for chartering singly or together, by the day or by the week.

33

CAPACITY

Reception: 48 to 150
Banquet: 100
Meeting: 100
(Larger groups can be handled in cooperation with Amtrak.)

LOCATION

American Zephyr's offices are located in downtown Washington, but you board the train at Union Station, a few blocks from the U.S. Capitol Building.

FOOD/BEVERAGE

American Zephyr offers a full bar service. You're free to choose your own caterer, although the staff will make suggestions, if requested.

LIMITATIONS/RESTRICTIONS

Moving functions, one-way or round trip, are coordinated with Amtrak schedules. In-station functions are offered only in Washington, D.C., Philadelphia, New York City and Boston.

LEAD TIME FOR RESERVATIONS

Ten days. The American Zephyr accepts reservations a year in advance.

RATES

In-station events: $35 per person, with a $1,750 minimum. This rate is for three-hour events and includes premium brand bar service. For dining and moving functions, contact American Zephyr.

FACILITIES FOR THE PHYSICALLY HANDICAPPED?
YES NO SOME
    X

THE BOYHOOD HOME OF ROBERT E. LEE

607 Oronoco Street
Alexandria, Virginia 22314
703/548-8454

Reserve a place in history

Those wide planks you tread upon when you enter this house may be the same floorboards the young Robert E. Lee crossed to welcome such guests as George Washington and the Marquis de Lafayette. When you stand, drink in hand, mingling in the beautiful boxwood garden, you're on the same ground that little Lee frolicked upon with his siblings and cousins. The future confederate general came to this 1795 Federal-style brick house at the age of five. He left it for West Point in 1825.

You get a tour of this historic house with your rental fee, but your event is confined to the grounds and the first floor foyer/dining room/winter-kitchen area. The dining room, like the rest of the dwelling, is decorated with Federal-period furniture. A portrait of Lee's father, Revolutionary War hero "Light Horse Harry" Lee, hangs over the fireplace mantel. Round tables are placed in the dining room for seated dinners, and the old winter kitchen at the back of the house serves as the bar area.

The foyer is itself a marvelous space. The high ceiling is decorated with a medallion engraving of intertwining tobacco leaves. An oriental rug lies across the floor and an archway gracefully slopes from one wall to the other.

If your event is scheduled for one of the warmer months, you'll enjoy the garden with its expansive lawn and boxwood-bordered brick paths. The tall magnolia tree is said to have been planted by Robert E. Lee's mother.

CAPACITY

Reception: 100 (summer months); 75 (winter months)
Banquet: 40
Garden party: 100
Luncheon: 40

LOCATION

One block east of George Washington Memorial Parkway (Washington Street within city limits) in Old Town Alexandria.

FOOD/BEVERAGE

You must choose a caterer from the staff's approved list. A modern kitchen is available and offers a warming oven and a refrigerator.

LIMITATIONS/RESTRICTIONS

Smoking and dancing are not allowed in the house. Food and drink are not allowed above the ground floor and the upstairs rooms are roped off. The music played must be in keeping with the style of the house. The house normally closes from the middle of December to the first of February, but special arrangements may be made to hold an event here during that time. Otherwise, the house is available any day of the week from 10:00 A.M. to 10:00 P.M.

LEAD TIME FOR RESERVATIONS

Call for availability.

RATES

$125 per hour. There is a two-hour minimum.

FACILITIES FOR THE PHYSICALLY HANDICAPPED?
YES NO SOME
   X

CABELL'S MILL

5235 Walney Road
Centreville, Virginia 22021
Mailing address: 5040 Walney Road
Chantilly, Virginia 22021
703/631-9566

Stone building by a stream

Who says that rustic has to be primitive? At Cabell's Mill it certainly isn't.

This sturdy, stone building set in a pretty Virginia park dates back to 1800 or so, when it was waterpowered to grind grain and later, to grind sumac. Water wheel and machinery are gone, but the natural setting remains the same: Big Rocky Run flows by and trees, shrubs, birds and flowers surround you. You can hold an event outside, if you like, or you can use the mill. One large upstairs room and a smaller room downstairs comprise the interior. The stone fireplace on each floor works, but the mill is also equipped with heating and air conditioning. Inside stone walls have been covered over with plaster and the overall feel here is of a modern facility. The rooms are mostly unfurnished, although a limited number of chairs and tables are included in the rental. Cabell's Mill offers a simple but gracious setting and is especially suited to groups with restricted budgets.

Cabell's Mill and the surrounding park grounds were given to the Fairfax County Park Authority by Ellanor C. Lawrence, whose husband was the founder and publisher of *U.S. News and World Report*. The Lawrences used Cabell's Mill as a guest house for visitors to their nearby Walney Farm.

CAPACITY

Reception: 150
Banquet: 70 to 80
Grounds: 150
Meetings: 75

LOCATION

From the Beltway: Take Exit 9 or 9A to Route 66 West; follow Route 66 eleven miles to Exit 13, Route 28; turn left on Route 28 and travel .1 mile to Walney Road; take a right on Walney Road and follow it one mile to the mill.

FOOD/BEVERAGE

You choose your own caterer. You need to purchase a banquet permit from the Virginia Alcoholic Beverage Control Commission to sell alcohol at the mill, but no permit is required serve it. A cooling kitchen is equipped with a sink and refrigerator.

LIMITATIONS/RESTRICTIONS

Smoking is prohibited in the mill and music must be kept to a reasonable volume. The mill is closed from the middle of January to the end of February.

LEAD TIME FOR RESERVATIONS

Weekdays: at least one month in advance.
Weekends: at least six months in advance.

RATES

The mill and grounds each rent for $100 for a six-hour period, plus a $150 refundable damage deposit. When you rent both the mill and the grounds, the cost is $150 for six hours, plus a $300 refundable damage deposit. Overtime charges run $40 an hour.

FACILITIES FOR THE PHYSICALLY HANDICAPPED?
YES NO SOME
X

CALVERT COLLECTION

2301 Calvert Street, N.W.
Washington, D.C. 20008
202/387-5177

A turn-of-the-century treasure house

Treat yourself to a look at the outside of the Calvert Collection mansion before you go in. It's a four-story, many-windowed, Queen Anne Revival structure wrapped around a corner. The house's placement gives it an expansive facade behind which the rest of the building gracefully tapers.

Its fine design creates a unique interior. Large, rectangular rooms lie in front while in back the rooms are smaller and often wedge-shaped. Altogether, there are 11 display rooms filled with an amazingly diverse collection of art and antiques. Ancient Japanese china, early American pine furniture, Italian Renaissance paintings and European sculpture are some of the pieces you may happen upon.

Any event you hold here is going to seem sumptuous, a tone set not only by the splendid collection but by such decorative flourishes as elaborate crystal chandeliers, huge mirrors, columns and thick red carpeting. The first floor is mainly a reception area, whereas the second, third and fourth floors are available for meetings (you can use one of the collection's antique tables for a conference table, if you want), cocktail receptions and banquets. If you feel nervous about making all the proper arrangements for your function, you can take advantage of the special event-planning and management services the staff offers.

The Calvert Collection building is also known as the Wickersham mansion. It was built in 1913 for Mrs. Turner A. Wickersham, a socialite who is said to have brought the Christian Science movement to Washington.

CAPACITY

Reception: 150
Banquet: 70

LOCATION

In upper northwest Washington, one block east of Connecticut Avenue; within walking distance of the Omni Shoreham and Sheraton Washington hotels.

FOOD/BEVERAGE

The Calvert Collection accepts all licensed caterers and provides the use of a full kitchen and service stairs.

LIMITATIONS/RESTRICTIONS

Amplified music is prohibited.

LEAD TIME FOR RESERVATIONS

Six to eight months. Early fall is the busiest time. Call for availability.

RATES

$1200 to $1,500, depending on length of function and the day of the week you reserve the house. (Holiday functions incur a 50 percent surcharge on the regular rental fee.)

FACILITIES FOR THE PHYSICALLY HANDICAPPED?
YES NO SOME
　　X

CARLYLE HOUSE

121 North Fairfax Street
Alexandria, Virginia 22314
703/549-2997

Old Town Alexandria's 235-year-old country manor

When you step through the door of the Carlyle House your first thought may be that someone's taken liberties with the interior decoration. You won't find demure Williamsburg blue and cranberry colors here. No, the walls and furniture are painted in shades of turquoise blue and emerald green. Experts have discovered that these were the fashionable decorating colors in the 1750s, when wealthy Scottish mer-

chant and leading citizen of Alexandria John Carlyle built his gorgeous Georgian structure.

For meeting, reception and banquet purposes, the brightly furnished rooms create a festive air. You can use the hallway, dining room and parlor on the first floor, the central hall on the second floor, and the brick terrace that overlooks the formal garden.

Indoor banquets and meetings most often take place in the parlor, a large room that somehow has managed to keep its original woodwork—graceful swan's neck pediments over the doorways and fine cornices. The halls on both floors are spacious areas; the upstairs hall actually was used as a bedroom in the mid-19th century, when the house served as a hotel. Other rooms on view but not for use include an unplastered room that exposes in layers the house's construction and restoration history, and Carlyle's magnificent bedroom on the first floor.

When you open the door at the back of the first floor hall, you step out onto the terrace balcony. In warm weather, this is a fantastic area in which to hold receptions and banquets. Right below you is the beautifully landscaped garden and beyond that, a few blocks, flows the Potomac River. In Carlyle's time the Potomac lapped at the back edge of his property.

CAPACITY

Reception: 100, inside; 150, with tent on the terrace.
Banquet: 35, inside; 80 to 100, with a tent on the terrace.
Meeting: 35, inside.

LOCATION

A few blocks east of the George Washington Memorial Parkway (Washington Street), in Old Town Alexandria.

FOOD/BEVERAGE

You can choose your own caterer. You must obtain a banquet permit if you're going to have a cash bar. There is no kitchen facility in the house.

LIMITATIONS/RESTRICTIONS

Smoking and dancing are prohibited in the house but are allowed on the terrace. Amplified music is not allowed. Events may take place from 6:30 P.M. to midnight. Caterers are allowed in at 5:30 P.M. but everyone, including caterers, must be gone by midnight. There are no Monday rentals. The terrace may be tented from April 15 to October 15. A tent is required when your party includes more than 100 people.

LEAD TIME FOR RESERVATIONS

Fall and spring months are the most popular, but call for availability.

RATES

$975, flat fee, plus $43.88 tax, plus a $225 refundable security deposit.

FACILITIES FOR THE PHYSICALLY HANDICAPPED?
YES NO SOME
         X

An outdoor lift can take you to the first floor only, from the lower level.

CHRISTIAN HEURICH MANSION

1307 New Hampshire Avenue, N.W.
Washington, D.C. 20036
202/785-2068

Victorian fortress in downtown Washington

It's safe to say that there isn't an unadorned space in all of the Christian Heurich Mansion. There are allegorical paintings on the ceilings, decorative brass grilles hiding the radiators, intricately carved wood panels encasing the fireplaces and gilding on the bathroom tiles. What you're seeing is the home of a wealthy German whose decorating tastes were influenced by the customs of his native country as well as his adopted country, trends in those Victorian times and his own indomitable personality.

Whether you throw a reception throughout all seven of the available first floor rooms or reserve the conservatory and garden for a banquet, you won't lack for conversation. The foyer recalls a medieval castle decorated as it is with a standing coat of armor, mosaic floor and silvered plaster medallions on the stucco walls.

The other first floor areas include a reception room, which is an experience in crimson; the "museum rooms": the formal blue parlor, gold parlor, and music room with an overhanging musicians' gallery; and a dining room whose walls, ceiling and furniture are carved of oak.

The conservatory behind the dining room presents an entirely different image from the rest of the house. This is the room frequently used for events, and no wonder—the terra-cotta and turquoise-colored tile floor, red-paned windows, bark-like wall coverings and small fountain create a pleasant and relaxing atmosphere.

The Victorian garden, too, is splendid for dinner parties and receptions. It is spacious, split attractively in the middle

44

by hedges, and features a brick patio that's a perfect spot for setting up the bar.

The Christian Heurich Mansion serves as the headquarters for the Columbia Historical Society.

CAPACITY

Reception: 100 (house), 200 (house and garden)
Banquet: 50 to 65 (house), 200 (house and garden)
Garden party: 150
Meeting: 40 to 60

LOCATION

At Dupont Circle in northwest Washington, within walking distance of the Dupont Circle Metro station.

FOOD/BEVERAGE

You can choose your own caterer, but the caterer must be bonded and insured. Caterers can use a ground floor kitchen and a first floor pantry for food preparation but not cooking or heating.

LIMITATIONS/RESTRICTIONS

Smoking is allowed only in the garden and the conservatory. You may serve and consume food and drink only in the conservatory and garden during the warm months; during the winter months, you may serve food in the dining room and carry drinks into the hall. Food and drink are never allowed in the three "museum" rooms. Amplified music is not allowed. The mansion is not air-conditioned. Tents are required in he garden when the number of your party exceeds 100. There is no parking on the premises, but the mansion includes in its rental information portfolio the names, numbers and hours of nearby parking garages.

LEAD TIME FOR RESERVATIONS

At least one month.

RATES

Rates range from $150 for a nonprofit organization's half-day meeting to $1,250 for a commercial organization's reception and dinner. If you rent the mansion in January, February, July or August you receive a 10 percent discount.

FACILITIES FOR THE PHYSICALLY HANDICAPPED?

Full handicapped facilities will be completed in 1989.

COLLINGWOOD-ON-THE-POTOMAC

The Collingwood Library and Museum on
Americanism
8301 East Boulevard Drive
Alexandria, Virginia 22308
703/765-1652

The house that George built

"If others talk at Table be attentive but talk not with Meat in your mouth." So wrote George Washington in his diary when he was a boy, along with more than 100 other such "Rules of Civility" our first president learned from his own translations from the French he did as a teenager. The full and humorous list is exhibited here at Collingwood.

As a library and museum on Americanism, Collingwood is fascinating. As a meeting site, it's delightful. Both floors of the white Federal Palladian structure are open to you. The downstairs library is painted sky blue and is furnished, as you might imagine, with many bookcases, display tables and cozy chairs placed here and there. You're free to walk around and peruse the materials, but food and drink are prohibited in these rooms.

The upstairs museum rooms offer a fine reception and banquet area. There is one large room and three adjoining smaller ones, all of which are filled with artifacts of our American heritage: state flags and military service flags, Revolutionary War mementos, a Hopi kachina doll and an Alaskan totem pole, to name a few. Other than the museum pieces, the rooms have little furniture, leaving plenty of room for setup tables and mingling space.

One of the remarkable things about this site is its location—it is literally on the Potomac. You can walk out the side door and down the long, sloping green lawn right to the river. The combination of nine green acres and a riverfront location make Collingwood one of the nicest places to have an outdoor affair.

Collingwood was once part of George Washington's river farm. The oldest part of the mansion dates to 1785 which Washington had built as the dwelling for one of his farm managers. Besides being a museum and library on Americanism, it is headquarters for the National Sojourners, a group of American veterans who are also Masons.

CAPACITY

Reception: 125 to 150
Banquet: 75
Garden party: 150 (special arrangements can be made to host larger parties)
Meeting: 75

LOCATION

Four miles south of Old Town Alexandria. From Washington, take the George Washington Memorial Parkway (Washington Street within the city limits) to the Mount Vernon Memorial Parkway. Take the Collingwood Road exit, turn left onto East Boulevard Drive, then right into the Collingwood property.

FOOD/BEVERAGE

You can choose your own caterer, subject to approval by the Collingwood Directors.

LIMITATIONS/RESTRICTIONS

Smoking is prohibited inside the building. Alcoholic beverages are limited to wine, beer and champagne. The site is available all year round except December 20 to January 5: after 4:00 P.M. for indoor and outdoor social functions, from 9:00 A.M. to 5:00 P.M. for indoor meetings.

LEAD TIME FOR RESERVATIONS

Call for availability.

RATES

From $400 to $1,000, depending on the type of function, type of organization renting and the number of guests.

FACILITIES FOR THE PHYSICALLY HANDICAPPED?
YES NO SOME
X

The first floor of the building is accessible to the handicapped, including its restrooms.

COLVIN RUN MILL

10017 Colvin Run Road
Great Falls, Virginia 22066
703/759-2771

Nothing run of the mill about it

As you pull off the road onto the site of Colvin Run Mill, the smell of honeysuckle and flowers replaces the smell of car fumes, and the soft sounds of birds chirping and water flowing replace the sounds of traffic. You're not very far from busy Leesburg Pike, but you'd never know it.

The large, three-story brick mill sits on a green expanse of grass, next to the creek that powers the mill. Ducks and geese flirt in the pond, the water wheel churns and peace reigns.

Two floors of the mill are yours for functions. Each floor features a wide-open room with worn, white oak floors; exposed heavy wood beamed ceilings and supports; and assorted mill apparatus. Some of the mill works are cleverly disguised; what you think is a wood column may be a grain elevator or a vertical drive shaft. The mill has been carefully restored to look and operate as it did around 1810, when Philip Carver, a local businessman, built it.

The thick brick walls of the mill, as well as its placement on the banks of Colvin Run, make it a dark, cool place, even on a hot summer evening. You're welcome to roam the grounds while you're here, or if you like, you may rent the grounds, either with the mill or without. A popular spot for outdoor affairs lies up the hill from the mill, nestled between the 19th-century general store and the miller's house.

CAPACITY

Reception: 150
Banquet: 150
Garden Party: 150

LOCATION

From the Beltway: Take Exit 10B to Route 7 West. Continue on Route 7 until you're five miles west of Tysons Corner. Turn right on Colvin Run Road.

FOOD/BEVERAGE

Catering, tables and chairs are all up to you. You'll need a banquet permit to serve or sell alcohol.

LIMITATIONS/RESTRICTIONS

Smoking and candles are not permitted in the mill. The mill is neither heated nor air-conditioned. The mill is available after 5:00 P.M., Friday through Sunday, from March 15 through October 31. Restrooms are located up the hill from the mill.

LEAD TIME FOR RESERVATIONS

At least three weeks, although staff recommends three months.

RATES

$250 for the mill, $150 for the grounds, for a four-hour period; $25 for each additional hour up to six hours. A $150 refundable security deposit is required. Rates may increase in 1988.

FACILITIES FOR THE PHYSICALLY HANDICAPPED?
YES NO SOME
X

50

THE DANDY

Potomac Party Cruises
Zero Prince Street
Alexandria, Virginia 22314
703/683-6076

For a dandy old time

You could say that *The Dandy* is Washington's answer to the Parisian riverboats that cruise the Seine. And what an answer it is! *The Dandy* is a floating restaurant/ballroom/tourmobile/meeting site.

The boat is a climate-controlled, all-weather, glassed-in cruise vessel. Its interior is furnished as a restaurant in tones of blue and burgundy. In the middle is a dance floor. A candlelit, four-hour evening cruise offers you a sumptuous five-course dinner, followed by dancing to taped music played over the boat's superb sound system. A two and one-half hour luncheon cruise offers you a delicious three-course meal and live entertainment provided by the singing captain and the Strolling Strings Trio. The highlight of a ride aboard *The Dandy* is the spectacular view you have of the monuments, Georgetown, the Kennedy Center and other Washington sights.

Private charters are available to groups for special events.

CAPACITY

Reception: 200
Banquet: 200
Meeting: 200

LOCATION

You board The Dandy *at its Prince Street pier, located in Old Town Alexandria. Follow the George Washington Memorial Parkway (Washington Street within city limits) to Duke Street and follow Duke Street to the waterfront. There are several parking lots near the pier. Prince Street is one block north of Duke Street.*

FOOD/BEVERAGE

The Dandy *is a restaurant that offers full-course meals for lunch and dinner.*

LIMITATIONS/RESTRICTIONS

There are no specific restrictions, but review your requirements with management.

LEAD TIME FOR RESERVATIONS

Call for availability. Large groups should plan further ahead than small ones, which can be combined with others.

RATES

Evening dinner/dance cruises: $40 per person Sunday through Thursday, $45 per person Friday and Saturday, plus bar charges, gratuities and sales tax.
Lunch cruises; $25 per person daily.
Special charters: call for rates.

FACILITIES FOR THE PHYSICALLY HANDICAPPED?
YES NO SOME
    X

DRANESVILLE TAVERN

11919 Leesburg Pike
Herndon, Virginia 22070
Mailing address: 10017 Colvin Run Road
Great Falls, Virginia 22066
703/759-2771

Stop in and stay awhile

Folks in earlier times never had it as good as you can today at Dranesville Tavern. Built in 1825 as a "drover's rest," that is, a stopping place for people on their way to market, Dranesville Tavern provided food, drink and a place to sleep. When you stop in at the Dranesville Tavern these days, you bring your own food and drink, but the tavern offers you the historic atmosphere and charm of its restored rooms, as well as such modern amenities as central heating and air conditioning.

You can use all nine rooms of the two-story tavern. There are few furnishings, but you do get little glimpses into the past—from a display board that explains the tavern's construction history, from small interior windows set in the wall that reveal layers of the structure, from the restored squash-colored and blue-green painted woodwork, and just from noticing the low ceilings and doorways that were typical of buildings in the days when Americans were generally shorter.

You are also welcome to rent the open grounds that surround the tavern.

CAPACITY

Reception: 90
Banquet: 65 to 70
Garden party: 75
Meeting: 35 in one room

LOCATION

From the Beltway, take Exit 10B (Tysons Corner, Route 7) and follow Route 7 west for ten miles. Dranesville Tavern will be on your left as you approach. Because there is no direct left turn lane into the tavern park, you must make a U-turn from the first left-turn lane on Route 7 just past the tavern, and then turn right onto the tavern property.

FOOD/BEVERAGE

Catering is left to you. A kitchen on the premises is equipped with outlets, a sink and refrigerator. A banquet license is required if you're going to serve or sell alcohol.

LIMITATIONS/RESTRICTIONS

Smoking and candles are prohibited in the tavern. The tavern is available March through December from 5:00 P.M. to midnight on Friday, and from noon to midnight, Saturday and Sunday.

LEAD TIME FOR RESERVATIONS

Anywhere from three weeks to four months, depending upon availability. The tavern's busiest months are November and December; its slowest months are March and April.

RATES

Tavern: $100 for a four-hour minimum, plus $25 for each additional hour, for a maximum of six hours. Grounds: $75 for a minimum of four hours, plus $25 for each additional hour, for a maximum of six hours. Tavern and grounds: $175 for a minimum of four hours, plus $25 for each additional hour, for a maximum of six hours.

FACILITIES FOR THE PHYSICALLY HANDICAPPED
YES NO SOME
   X

FONDO DEL SOL

Visual Art and Media Center
2112 R Street, N.W.
Washington, D.C. 20008
202/483-2777

A celebration of America's varied cultures

You don't have to travel all the way to South or Central America to enjoy yourselves in true Latino fashion. Hold an event at Fondo del Sol and you can tango Argentina, sway to salsa and reggae, admire Hispanic-oriented art and feast on exotic foods such as pollo asada and ceviche.

You know you've found Fondo del Sol when you spot the red banner displaying a golden sun that hangs over the entrance to the white Victorian townhouse. Inside, there are four rooms on two floors, the entrance hall and a small garden available for use. The front room on each floor features a windowed bay that seems suitable as a setup spot. Overall, the interior is plain, directing your attention to the multi-cultural art displayed throughout. Half of the gallery's exhibitions showcase the works of Latino artists; the other half feature the works of Native Americans, Afro-Americans, ethnic Americans and others.

Fondo del Sol specializes in making an event come alive through festive presentations of music, dance and unusual dishes. This is the sort of place where parties often spill into the street. To make sure the good time lasts forever, Fondo del Sol will also videotape your event for you.

Founded in 1973, Fondo del Sol is the nation's second largest Spanish-speaking and Hispanic-oriented museum.

CAPACITY

Reception: 100 to 150
Banquet: 60
Meeting: 35 to 40 in one room

LOCATION:

In the Dupont Circle area of northwest Washington, seven minutes' walk from the Dupont Circle Metro station at Q Street, N.W.

FOOD/BEVERAGE

Fondo del Sol will cater your event for you or allow you to make your own arrangements. A small kitchen is available.

LIMITATIONS/RESTRICTIONS

Fondo del Sol is closed in August. The center is available the rest of the year Tuesdays through Saturdays, from 9:00 A.M. to 1:00 P.M. and from 5:30 P.M. to midnight, and all day on Mondays.

LEAD TIME FOR RESERVATIONS

At least a month.

RATES

From $200 for a simple cocktail party to $5,000 for an event provided with music, food and video services.

FACILITIES FOR THE PHYSICALLY HANDICAPPED?
YES NO SOME
    X

GADSBY'S TAVERN

138 North Royal Street
Alexandria, Virginia 22314
703/548-1288

Hot spot in colonial times

As you collect your colleagues around you at Gadsby's Tavern, you're carrying on a tradition that goes back to 1770, when the tavern was built. Just as you have chosen an unbusinesslike setting in which to discuss the news of the day, work-related or otherwise, so did our founding fathers.

Today's tavern building originally housed Gadsby's City Hotel, but its three rooms have been restored to replicate the meeting rooms of the Hotel Breeches. Food, serving pieces, furnishings and costumes recall colonial times.

In the Tap Room, you'll find a barkeep dressed in britches, billowing shirt and vest dispensing drinks through the window of the wooden bar enclosure in the back corner. The cozy room exudes a convivial atmosphere with its well-worn floor, fireplace, an antique desk or two, hurricane lamps, square wooden tables and old chairs.

Adjoining the Tap Room are the warm, but slightly more formal, dining rooms. You'll see the same wide-planked floor and square tables found in the bar, but other touches, such as blue Roman window shades and the pistachio-green painted woodwork, enhance the decor. You'll chuckle at the Hogarth reproductions hanging on the walls, depicting scenes of drunken revelry.

A courtyard behind the tavern is also available during the warmer months, with the rental of the tavern rooms or for regular dining. This space originally served as the coachyard for the tavern. Three old coach sheds still stand and one of them may be used as the bar for receptions.

Trees and shrubs and a large white canopy help to make this a shaded and attractive spot for parties.

CAPACITY

Reception: 175, with courtyard
Banquet: 90
Garden party: 50

LOCATION

A few blocks east of the George Washington Memorial Parkway (Washington Street within the city limits) and one block north of King Street in Old Town Alexandria.

FOOD/BEVERAGE

The tavern caters all events and features mostly colonial-style food (for example, "colonial cheese pasties" and "George Washington's favorite duck"). Menus are available.

LIMITATIONS/RESTRICTIONS

Only period music is allowed, and amplified music is prohibited. The tavern can help you find musicians who play period music.

LEAD TIME FOR RESERVATIONS

Four to five days.

RATES

Entire tavern, plus courtyard: $500; main dining room $225; back dining room: $110; tap room: $165. The entire tavern may be rented for a three-hour period, from 2:30 P.M. to 5:30 P.M. or from 3 P.M. to 6 P.M., Saturdays and Sundays only. Individual rooms can be rented from 5:30 P.M. to 8:30 P.M. or from 8:30 P.M. on, any day of the week. These rates do not include meal and bar charges. The average cost per plate is $15.

FACILITIES FOR THE PHYSICALLY HANDICAPPED?
YES NO SOME
X

H.H. LEONARDS FINE ARTS MANSION

2020 O Street, N.W.
Washington, D.C. 20036
202/659-8787

Off-the-wall art in a Victorian home

You'll probably feel as if you're in someone's private home when you hold an event at H.H. Leonards Fine Arts Mansion. That's because it *is* a private home—H.H and family actually live in this furnished, four-story Victorian. Unlike a party at a friend's house, however, you don't have to covet a furnishing silently or ask the hostess where she purchased it. You can buy it. Everything you see here is for sale, from the paintings in the bathrooms to the bed on which H.H. sleeps.

Rambles around the entire house come with the rental of the site. Art and antiques lovers will be in ecstasy over the more than 5,000 art objects on view, including paintings, sculpture, glasswork, pottery, chandeliers, china, sofas, mirrors and countless other items.

Aside from the art, the house itself might be considered an art object. It dates from 1892 and features all the original woodwork—and there is a lot of it. Cherry-wood paneling frames a big picture window in the front drawing room, and oak paneling embellishes the entranceways, walls and fireplaces throughout the rest of the house. The most magnificent room is the dining room. A huge, floor-to-ceiling, built-in oak buffet gives prominence to the colorful Tiffany window at its center. A built-in china hutch sits in one corner; a fireplace fits snugly in the other.

H.H. Leonards is an art consultant as well as an art dealer. She advises business people and individuals about investing in art. Groups approved by H.H. to hold special events here will enjoy not only the captivating setting but also, perhaps, a private lesson in the value of art.

CAPACITY

Reception: 100
Banquet: 60
Meeting: 60

LOCATION

In the Dupont Circle area of Washington, two blocks from the Dupont Circle Metro station.

FOOD/BEVERAGE

H.H. Leonards, Inc., handles all your catering needs.

LEAD TIME FOR RESERVATIONS

Call for availability.

RATES

Rates range from $25 to $250 per person, depending upon the type of event you're planning. What do you get for $250?— what do you want?

FACILITIES FOR THE PHYSICALLY HANDICAPPED?
YES NO SOME
　　　X

HUNTER HOUSE

9601 Courthouse Road
Vienna, Virginia 22180
703/938-7532

A landmark site and recreational facility

Tennis, anyone? Yes, if you want, you can play tennis, baseball, soccer or basketball, follow an exercise fitness trail or simply take a hike—in addition to holding a gracious affair at the mansion here.

Hunter House is a cream-colored, brown-trimmed frame structure that lies within the 84-acre Nottaway Park. A ground-floor hall and a large room that opens onto a screened-in side porch are the spaces available to you inside the mansion. White walls, high ceilings, recessed lights and polished pine floors add luster to unfurnished rooms.

A flagstone path leads from Hunter House's back door to its secluded lawn, a tree-shaded area bordered by gardens and shrubs. The park's recreational facilities are just far enough away so that rebel yells and cheerleading don't disturb your function.

Now the property of the Fairfax County Park Authority, Hunter House was built in 1890 and served first as a residence for Scottish immigrant John Hunter and later as part of a winery.

CAPACITY

Reception: 75 (inside), 125 (with canopy on back lawn)
Banquet: 50 (inside), 125 (with canopy on back lawn)
Garden party: 125
Meeting: 50

LOCATION

From the Beltway: Take Exit 9 or 9A (Route 66 West) to right on Route 243 (Nutley Street) to left on Courthouse Road to park entrance on left.

FOOD/BEVERAGE

Hunter House offers you its approved list of caterers; you can choose from this list or from one of your own. A kitchen is available with a dishwasher, counter space and refrigerator.

LIMITATIONS/RESTRICTIONS

Smoking is prohibited inside the house. When the number of your party exceeds the house's maximum of 75, you are required to rent a tent. A liquor permit is required if you plan to serve alcohol. Alcohol is not permitted outside the house.

LEAD TIME FOR RESERVATIONS

Up to a year.

RATES

Rates range from $10 for a $3\frac{1}{2}$ hour meeting inside the house to $170 for the use of the grounds and the house for a four-hour function. Overtime charges are $10 an hour for county residents and $20 an hour for nonresidents. An alcoholic beverage use permit is $30 for county residents and $60 for nonresidents. The house is available all year, from 8:00 A.M. to midnight.

FACILITIES FOR THE PHYSICALLY HANDICAPPED?
YES NO SOME
X

LEE-FENDALL HOUSE

614 Oronoco Street

Alexandria, Virginia 22314

703/548-1789

House at Lee Corner

One thing you're sure to learn by renting the Lee-Fendall House is that Alexandria is indeed an old town and the Lees, one of the town's more prominent founding families. This house was built in 1785 and Lees lived here continuously until 1903. George Washington liked to drop in for a visit from time to time, along with his friend and Revolutionary War hero "Light Horse Harry" Lee.

Receptions, lunches, dinners and meetings take place in the dining room, central hallways (upstairs and down), sunporch and garden of the white clapboard structure. The garden is an especially attractive setting in spring when azaleas, roses and begonias bloom amidst the ancient ginko and chestnut trees. The interior is alluring all year round and is furnished as it was in Victorian times. Almost everything you see, from the baby carriage under the stairs to the 1840 Chickering piano in the drawing room, are Lee family heirlooms.

An intimate dinner in the antique-filled dining room can be an elegant candlelit affair conjuring up the spirits of the 37 Lees who have lived here. The large hallways are perfect cocktail reception spaces; when you need a break from mingling you can simply slip off to one of the surrounding rooms to peer at period furnishings. (You can't walk through these rooms but you can view them from the roped-off area just inside the door.)

Docents in colonial or Victorian dress are available to answer your questions about the Lees and the house. If you ask about the elevator, for example, you'll learn that it was installed by labor leader John L. Lewis when he lived here.

CAPACITY

Reception: 100
Banquet: 20
Garden party: 100
Meeting: 20

LOCATION

In Old Town Alexandria, at the corner of the George Washington Memorial Parkway (Washington Street) and Oronoco Street.

FOOD/BEVERAGE

You may choose your own caterer or use a caterer from the site's preferred list. A kitchen equipped with a stove but no refrigerator or freezer is available.

LIMITATIONS/RESTRICTIONS

Smoking is prohibited inside the house. Amplified music is prohibited outside. Events must end by 11:00 P.M.

LEAD TIME FOR RESERVATIONS

April/May and September/October are the most popular months. The site accepts reservations a year in advance; call for availability.

RATES

A flat fee of $115 per hour.

FACILITIES FOR THE PHYSICALLY HANDICAPPED?
YES NO SOME
    X

THE LYCEUM

201 South Washington Street
Alexandria, Virginia 20314
703/838-4994

A meeting place then and now

Back in the 1840s, you might have gathered at the Lyceum with fellow Alexandrians to listen to concerts and debates, and speeches by the likes of John Quincy Adams. The Lyceum serves equally well today as a place to gather for receptions, banquets, meetings and performances.

"An ornament to our town," declared *The Alexandria Gazette* about the Lyceum shortly after the building was constructed in 1839. The massive white brick and stucco building is of Doric temple design, fronting Old Town's busiest street with four impressive columns. The interior, however, is modern.

You can rent both floors of the Lyceum, although most groups find that the grand, second-floor auditorium best suits their purposes. The hall boasts a very high ceiling, in which many recessed lights are lodged. There is little in the way of decoration but a lot in the way of meeting accessories. Two pianos, a platform stage, projection booth, descending screen and controlled lighting are available if you need them.

Three museum rooms on the first floor house exhibits related to Alexandria's rich heritage and serve well as a reception area.

CAPACITY

Reception: 180
Banquet: 150
Meeting/Concert: 165 to 175

LOCATION

Three miles south of National Airport, on the George Washington Memorial Parkway (Washington Street) in Old Town Alexandria.

FOOD/BEVERAGE

You're free to choose your own caterer. A kitchen provides a refrigerator but no heating facility.

LIMITATIONS/RESTRICTIONS

Smoking is permitted only in the restrooms and outer lobbies. Music is allowed, but no hard rock or amplified music. Dancing is prohibited. (This restriction may be lifted in 1988.)

LEAD TIME FOR RESERVATIONS

Call for availability.

RATES

From $50 to $450, depending on the function. Security and cleanup charges are extra. When you rent the entire building, there's an additional fee, but you must call the Lyceum for that information.

FACILITIES FOR THE PHYSICALLY HANDICAPPED?
YES NO SOME
X

MONTPELIER MANSION

On Muirkirk Road, off of Route 197
Laurel, Maryland 20708
301/953–1376

Meet in the wings, mingle in the garden

You can't spend the night at Montpelier, as George Washington did 200 years ago on his way to and from the Constitutional Convention, but you can hold meetings and social events here. When you do, you'll find the mansion the same "large, Hndsome [sic], Elegant House" that Abigail Adams did in 1800.

Before you go indoors, however, you're going to be captivated by Montpelier's splendid garden. Surrounding the mansion is a beautifully maintained presentation of 150-year-old boxwoods, sugar-, Japanese- and red-maple trees, old magnolias, white ash trees and sprawling dogwoods. The lawn is available with the use of the house for outdoor functions or just for strolling.

There are five parts to the Georgian-style, symmetrically balanced building: the central portion, two hyphens (that is, the passages connecting the house to its wings), and then the east and west wings. The two, unfurnished wing rooms and a smaller room that was once the Gentleman's Parlor are the indoor rental areas. The wing rooms are peach-colored, hexagonally shaped, with nonworking fireplaces and doors leading to brick terraces. The Gentleman's Parlor is painted a period green and is used most often for bar or food setups.

You have access to the rest of the house for a walk-through tour while you're here. The roped-off rooms you'll see are furnished according to the styles of the 1830s, including the formal dining room, with its ornately carved fireplace and an original corner hutch.

Montpelier was built by Major Thomas Snowden, a Revolutionary War officer and descendant of a wealthy Welsh family that had arrived in Maryland in the mid-1600s.

CAPACITY

Reception: 100
Banquet: 100
Garden Party: 100
Meeting: 50

LOCATION

From the Beltway: Take the Baltimore-Washington Parkway North exit and travel on the parkway to Route 197. Take a left on Route 197 and go left again at the traffic light onto Muirkirk Road.

FOOD/BEVERAGE

The caterer is of your choosing. A warming/cooling kitchen is available.

LIMITATIONS/RESTRICTIONS

Smoking is permitted only in the wing rooms. Live amplified music is prohibited.

LEAD TIME FOR RESERVATIONS

One year for events scheduled for April, May, June, September or October; six months for events scheduled for other months, but call for availability.

RATES

Day meetings (8:00 A.M. to 3:00 P.M.): $60; evening meetings (3:00 P.M. to 11:00 P.M.): $100. Meeting rates cover a three-hour period and allow you the use of one of the wing rooms. Meetings lasting longer than three hours or meetings at which food and/or alcoholic beverages are served are considered special functions and are billed as such.

Special function rates cover a six-hour period and are as follows: Prince George's county residents—$270 for 55 people or less, plus $50 per hour over six hours; $420 for 55 to 100 people, plus $80 per hour over six hours. Nonresidents—$400 for 55 people or less, plus $75 per hour over six hours; $600 for 55 to 100 people, plus $120 per hour over six hours. These rates include the use of the garden and the use of two rooms (for social functions of up to 55 people) or the use of all three rentable areas on the first floor (for social functions of 55 to 100 people). Rates may change in 1989. Montpelier is a facility of the Maryland National Capital Park and Planning Commission.

FACILITIES FOR THE PHYSICALLY HANDICAPPED?
YES NO SOME
X

MOUNT VERNON COLLEGE

2100 Foxhall Road, N.W.
Washington, D.C. 20007
202/331-3538

Treasured spaces on campus

Maybe you thought you were through with school, but Mount Vernon College gives you two good reasons to return, if only for an afternoon or evening: its lovely Hand Chapel and the distinguished Post Hall.

The Florence Hollis Hand Chapel is an award winner, literally. Its design won an American Institute of Architects Honor Award in 1971. Situated as it is in a wooded ravine, the building is entered at ground level; you descend stairs to arrive at the chapel area. There you find light wood pews stacked theater-style around three sides of a center stage at the bottom. The fourth wall is all window and presents you with a soothing scene of trees and stream. Skylights positioned in the chapel's sloped ceiling allow events to take place in natural light. Hand Chapel is known for its fine acoustics and is best suited for meetings, lectures and performances, and, of course, worship services. A Steinway piano and an organ are available.

A different kind of place altogether, but just a short walk away, is Post Hall. The large, one-room hall is a gift left by Post Cereals heiress and Mount Vernon alumna Marjorie Merriweather Post, in honor of her parents.

The refined tone of Post Hall is set by the treasures you find in it: English Regency crystal and bronze chandeliers, a collection of early American glass, Georgian-style furniture and heirloom oriental rugs. There are long windows on the side walls, and french doors lead to a patio that overlooks the 26-acre campus. Post Hall is available for receptions, seminars and banquets.

CAPACITY

Reception: 150
Banquet: 70
Meeting: 100 (Post Hall), 250 (Hand Chapel)
Concert: 250

LOCATION

Five miles from the White House, on Foxhall and W Streets, N.W.

FOOD/BEVERAGE

The college handles all food and beverage service. Only light refreshments are permitted in the chapel. A small kitchen adjoins Post Hall.

LIMITATIONS/RESTRICTIONS

The two facilities are available all year, any day or evening, subject to the college's own schedule.

LEAD TIME FOR RESERVATIONS

About six to nine months. The college frequently uses these spots for its own affairs.

RATES

Post Hall: $300 per day. Hand Chapel: $400 per day. Special conference rates are available.

FACILITIES FOR THE PHYSICALLY HANDICAPPED?
YES NO SOME
X

Post Hall is accessible to the handicapped; Hand Chapel is not.

NEWTON WHITE MANSION

2708 Enterprise Road
Mitchellville, Maryland 20716
301/249-2004

A little bit of the unexpected

You expect a meeting/entertainment site to possess certain qualities—an attractive setting, room to accommodate you, adaptability to suit your purposes, a convenient location— that sort of thing. What you can't always count on is personality. The Newton White Mansion delivers on all scores.

You may have seen stone lions or dogs poised at the gateways to grand estates; here, your arrival is marked by a brick rooster atop one brick column and a brick hen crowning the other. Standing in sharp contrast to the mansion's proper Georgian facade is its front door, which is painted a pretty blue color usually found inside a house. Throughout the interior, you'll notice a fine, bleached pine paneling instead of the more common dark-wood paneling. Wall murals depicting bucolic farm scenes mix with a stylized art deco design in the dining room. Even the mansion's setting is a surprise—the rolling hills surrounding you are actually part of the adjoining golf course. (Games are on a first-come, first-served basis, if you're interested in playing a round.)

You have the use of the first floor and the grounds when you rent the estate. First floor rooms include a dining room and adjoining enclosed porch, the long central hall, the study, a large ballroom and an adjoining back room, and a screened-in sunporch.

In addition to its unusual features, the Newton White Mansion offers you beautiful versions of the usual features as well. Full-length windows are hung with balloon curtains and overlook the grounds. Crystal chandeliers light the ballroom. French doors in each of the first floor rooms at the back of the house lead to a large brick patio. The paneled fireplaces in the ballroom and study are functional.

Built in 1939, this house was once the home of Captain

74

White, who was the first commanding officer of the World War II aircraft carrier *USS Enterprise*.

CAPACITY

Reception: 200 (throughout the first floor)
Banquet: 80 (in one room), 120 (throughout the first floor)
Garden party: 200 standing, 120 seated
Meeting: 80 to 90 in one room

LOCATION

From downtown Washington: Take US Route 50 (John Hanson Highway) east to Route 704 north, the first exit beyond I-95 (Washington Beltway). Route 704 joins Route 450. Turn right on Route 450. Turn right on Route 193 (Enterprise Road) and travel approximately 3 miles. Turn right onto the Enterprise Estate grounds.

FOOD/BEVERAGE

You choose your own caterer. The mansion offers a large warming and cooling kitchen equipped with a 400-pound ice machine.

LIMITATIONS/RESTRICTIONS

No specific restrictions; discuss your requests with management.

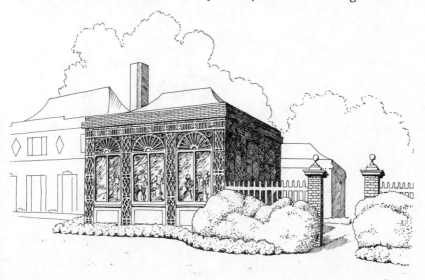

LEAD TIME FOR RESERVATIONS

The mansion starts accepting reservations one year in advance.

RATES

Weekdays: $20 per hour for nonprofit organizations, $40 per hour for profit organizations. Monday through Thursday evenings: $450 for a seven-hour period. Friday and Sundays: $700 for a seven-hour period. Saturdays: $850 for a seven-hour period. $300 security deposit (refundable).

FACILITIES FOR THE PHYSICALLY HANDICAPPED?
YES NO SOME
   X

There are plans to make the mansion accessible to the handicapped.

THE OCTAGON

1799 New York Avenue, N.W.
Washington, D.C. 20006
202/638-3105

Six sides, sixteen rooms and a garden

Take notice, all you meeting planner mavens! The Octagon, headquarters of the American Institute of Architects, is going to enrapture you and your gang. It's an historical, an architectural and a meeting place marvel.

When you rent the Federal-style mansion for a reception, banquet or garden party, you have access to the first two floors and the garden. You'll realize quickly that there are actually six sides to the house, not eight, and its unique shape creates a graceful interior. (The original owners, the Tayloe family, referred to their house as the Octagon and that's how it got its name.) Through the large, circular entry hall, you find yourself in another hall area that's dominated by an oval staircase curving continuously to the third floor. Extending diagonally off this middle ground are a dining room and a drawing room.

On the second floor are galleries displaying exhibits on architecture and the decorative arts. Above the circular foyer is the Treaty Room, which features the table on which President Madison is said to have signed the Treaty of Ghent ending the War of 1812. (This room is roped off.) After the British burned the White House in 1814, James and Dolley Madison lived in the Octagon while the President's home was being rebuilt. The wealthy Tayloes retreated to their Virginia plantation.

Besides the treaty table, there are many other original furnishings here. Note especially the Regency-style settee and armchair in the stair-hall, the gray and white marble floor in the central foyer and the Coade stone fireplace mantels in the dining and drawing rooms.

One other space in the house is available for luncheons and meetings, and that is the third-floor room known as Mrs. Ogle's parlor (Mrs. Ogle was Mrs. Tayloe's mother). Placed in line with the central entry hall, the room is perfectly round. It is painted in cheery yellow and blue and has a stunning view of the city.

Seated banquets are permitted in the garden area only, and may be held here all year round, with the use of a tent.

CAPACITY

Reception: 150 (inside), 200 (with a tented garden)
Banquet: 150 (only in the tented garden)
Lunch/meeting: 30

LOCATION

Two blocks west of the White House.

FOOD/BEVERAGE

The Octagon provides a list of suggested caterers and tent suppliers and you may choose from that list.

LIMITATIONS/RESTRICTIONS

Smoking and red wine are prohibited in the mansion. Seated dinners take place only in the tented garden. You may rent the Octagon if you are a 501(c)3—nonprofit—organization, a trade organization or a business.

LEAD TIME FOR RESERVATIONS

At least one month's notification is required with a nonrefundable 50 percent deposit given at time of booking. The Octagon accepts only 10 to 15 bookings each year, so call well in advance if you want to hold your event here.

RATES

Reception: $1,500; lunch: $500; garden dinner: $1,500. Catering and tent fees are not included in these rates. Rates may increase in 1988.

FACILITIES FOR THE PHYSICALLY HANDICAPPED?
YES NO SOME
X

The first floor and the garden are accessible to the handicapped.

RIVERSDALE

4811 Riverdale Road

Riverdale, Maryland 20737

301/779-2011

A Belgian's legacy to America

You won't see many mansions like Riversdale in the United States. Its 1801 architecture is a rare combination of Belgian and early 19th-century American features. The Belgian influence is most evident in the first floor parlor rooms, which were patterned after owner Henri Joseph Stier's chateau in Antwerp. Overall, the house is of Georgian design, following a plan created by architect Benjamin Henry Latrobe.

The rooms available to you when you rent the house are, in fact, the three Belgian-styled parlor rooms and a fourth room that once served as a carriage house. The parlors adjoin all in a row through wide entryways, which make it seem as if you're in one large salon. Fourteen-foot-high ceilings, finely carved cornices, oak floors and marble fireplaces grace each room. Rounded, floor-to-ceiling Belgian windows in the middle room lead to an outdoor marble terrace. The triple-arch motif that decorates the walls of this central salon were intended to frame works from the Baron's collection of Old World paintings, including some by Peter Paul Rubens, to whom he was related.

The fourth room, with its 19-foot-high ceiling and pine floor, serves best as a ballroom, although you may hold any sort of function here. On your way to this hall, you pass a glass-protected display of 1814, hand-blocked French wallpaper original to the house. A door in the ex-carriage house leads to the grounds, which you are free to roam.

Mr. Stier and his wife, who had come to the United States to escape the French Revolution, lived at Riversdale for less than a year before returning to their chateau in Antwerp. Instead, the Baron's daughter, Rosalie, and her husband, George Calvert, a descendant of Lord Baltimore, occupied Riversdale. Ownership of the estate passed from the Calvert family in 1887 to a number of other proprietors until, in 1949, the Maryland-National Capital Park and Planning Commission bought it. The Commission has plans underway to restore the mansion to its 1821 appearance. Riversdale will be closed during the course of the restoration, which began at the end of 1987 and will conclude in 1990. Areas of the house available for public use will change due to the restoration.

CAPACITY

Reception: 165
Banquet: 105
Meeting: 80

LOCATION

Between Route 1 and Kenilworth Avenue on Riverdale Road. About 15 miles from downtown Washington.

FOOD/BEVERAGE

A catering kitchen is included in restoration plans. Professional catering service may be required.

LIMITATIONS/RESTRICTIONS

Alcohol may be served, but not sold. Live amplified music is prohibited.

LEAD TIME FOR RESERVATIONS

Call for availability.

RATES

Prince George's County residents: reception—$550; banquet— $350; meeting—$70. Non-residents: reception—$800; banquet—$500; meeting—$70. Rates cover a six-hour period for receptions and banquets and three hours for meetings. Rates may increase after the completion of the renovation.

FACILITIES FOR THE PHYSICALLY HANDICAPPED?
YES NO SOME
X

After the renovation, Riversdale will have full facilities for the physically handicapped.

ROCKWOOD MANOR PARK

11001 MacArthur Boulevard
Potomac, Maryland 20854
301/585-5563

Camp cum conference center

Mention the name Rockwood to a Girl Scout and she'll tell
you it's a Girl Scout camp. That's what it used to be—a
national camp site that welcomed 15,000 to 20,000 Scouts
yearly. So it may surprise you to learn that the park has
taken on a new life as a classy conference center since a
major renovation by its new owners, the Maryland-National
Capital Park and Planning Commission.

Rockwood offers you a rambling brick manor house with
seven multi-purpose rooms and eight guest bedrooms, and
five separate overnight cabins, all situated in a private and
carefully maintained park.

The first thing you notice about the manor house interior
is that it is decorated throughout in shades of blue and
purple. The smallest of these blue rooms is the Girl Scout
Room, which accommodates 15, theater-style, and is filled
with historic Girl Scout memorabilia. Brooke Hall, an informal dining room with a linoleum floor, paneled vaulted
ceiling and brick fireplace, is the largest room, accommodating 132 for conferences and 50 for a banquet. Right next
door to Brooke Hall is the blue-carpeted Executive Dining
Room, which can handle 112 for presentations, 39 for a
banquet.

Loveliest of all is the Hoover Room, which seems best
suited for receptions. This high-ceilinged space is empty
but for its grand chandelier, working fireplace and mauve
carpet. French doors close off the room on one side; when
they are left open, the room becomes an upstairs gallery
overlooking the sunporch area below, known as the Ra-
padan Retreat.

Cabin accommodations vary from bright, homey bedrooms with private baths to dormitory dwellings with bunk

beds and central bathrooms. Rockwood is an ideal setting for small, corporate retreats and provides slide, film and video equipment to help with presentations.

CAPACITY

Reception: 150
Banquet: 89 (with 50 in one room and 39 in the adjoining room)
Meeting: 8 to 132
Accommodations: 129

LOCATION

Near Great Falls Park and within walking distance of the C&O Canal in southwestern Montgomery County, Maryland.

FOOD/BEVERAGE

You must choose a caterer from Rockwood's approved list. Alcohol is permitted, but you must obtain a license to serve or sell it.

LIMITATIONS/RESTRICTIONS

Amplified music is prohibited outside. Parking is limited to 60 spaces.

LEAD TIME FOR RESERVATIONS

The site accepts reservations one year in advance, but call for availability.

RATES

Conference room rates range from $35 for rental of the smallest room, to $675 for rental of all conference rooms and lounges, except for Brooke Hall. Lodging room rates range from $45 per night for a single room, to $825 per night for all 13 guest bedrooms, plus the use of the conference rooms and lounges. Dormitory rates range from $5 a person for one night to $576 for the use of all three dormitory buildings. Rates are likely to increase in 1988.

FACILITIES FOR THE PHYSICALLY HANDICAPPED?
YES NO SOME
X

ROSSBOROUGH INN

University of Maryland
Route 1
College Park, Maryland 20742
301/454-3940

A place to eat, meet and be merry

As you cruise down Route 1 toward the Rossborough, you may question whether there really is a historic, Federal-style mansion mixed in among the fast food joints and record stores. Keep going. This 1804 inn belongs to the University of Maryland and lies at the gateway to the campus.

Once you enter the Rossborough, you know you're in the right place. An air of history and hospitality pervades.

On the main floor is an elegant parlor where Lafayette once dined. A smoky blue carpet, Williamsburg blue-and-white painted walls, brass chandeliers and handsome table settings create a refined meeting area. Across the antique-laden hallway is the rustic tap room, a casual combination of old-fashioned bar, wood floor, tables and chairs. On one wall hangs an original survey map of the site, dating from 1793.

Up a wide, blue-carpeted staircase, you find five smaller rooms named for people who are connected with the inn or the college. The Ross room, for example, is named for the original owner of the home, and the Calvert room is named for a later owner who sold the inn to the state of Maryland at the end of the 19th century. Each room offers variations on the same theme: a pleasing color scheme, early American decor and private dining accommodations for small groups.

Connected by a covered walkway to the inn is a carriage house. With its worn brick floor, working fireplace and exposed beams, this one-room building is a natural for informal social gatherings.

If you're planning a spring or summer fling, you'll also want to know about the inn's garden. It has open hedges, a huge magnolia tree and a view of the campus.

CAPACITY

Reception: 150
Banquet: 75
Garden party: 150 to 200

LOCATION

Seven miles from the U.S. Capitol, on Route 1 across from the Ritchie Coliseum.

FOOD/BEVERAGE

The inn caters all functions and provides a catering guide upon request.

LIMITATIONS/RESTRICTIONS

The Rossborough Inn is primarily a restaurant and requires you to order food and beverage for your function. All-day business meetings are not allowed. A minimum of 40 people is required for evening functions. The Rossborough is not available on Sundays.

LEAD TIME FOR RESERVATIONS

At least two weeks. Large receptions should be booked one month in advance.

RATES

Tap room: $108; parlor: $120; carriage house: $184; second-floor rooms: from $24 to $48 each. Entire house: $372. These rates cover a three-hour period. A $1 per person overtime rate is charged when your event runs longer than three hours. Menu rates range from $11.95 to $18.50 per person.

FACILITIES FOR THE PHYSICALLY HANDICAPPED?
YES NO SOME
   X

SAM PARDOE'S HOUSE

2804 Q Street, N.W.
Washington, D.C. 20036
Mailing address: WashingtonInc.
1990 M Street, N.W., Suite 310
Washington, D.C. 20036
202/828-7000

Fun and games in a Georgetown mansion

If you've ever been to Georgetown, you know that it's a neighborhood of two personalities. The main streets are lined with shops selling all the latest and most innovative clothing, music, food and hairstyles. Follow a side street back, however, and you discover a historic and quainter Georgetown of private, narrow, tree-lined avenues, unevenly paved brick sidewalks and well-preserved old townhouses. Like the neighborhood in which you find it, Sam Pardoe's Georgetown mansion is a happy meshing of these two personalities.

The house itself is not old—it was built in 1980; nevertheless, its red brick, neo-Federal design blends right in with the senior structures surrounding it. It looks . . . traditional. Ah, but looks can be deceiving!

Consider the innovations first (everyone else does). At the end of the entrance hall, whose walls are covered with ultrasuede, is the living room. Not just any living room. This one is the bottom layer of an atrium that cuts up through the center of the house to the third floor. Recessed in the cathedral ceiling are multi-colored lights that can be programmed to beam with the beat of music.

Over in a corner is a brass fireman's pole that descends from the third floor (Pardoe uses it but you may not). You can travel floor to floor via a smoked glass elevator, similar to those installed in hotels. In another corner is a small, handsomely paneled English bar. Flip a switch and a flower-patterned stained glass door moves out of its hiding place in the wall to close off the bar. On the other side of the living room, three sets of French doors lead to a private brick-paved porch, patio and mini reflecting pool.

Take a moment to visit the powder room off the entrance hall. Place your hands close to the faucets. Presto! The temperature-controlled water turns on, nudged electronically. Take your hands away and the water turns off.

Other fun gadgets await you upstairs (like the toy train that charges around a track set close to the ceiling in the library), but now let's talk about those things that make the Pardoe house refined as well as fun.

On the first floor, you'll find 100-year-old hardwood covering the floors and century-old brick covering one whole wall of the living room. Antique furnishings include a 300-year-old highboy, and an old wood chest hand-carved by Pardoe's mother. On the second floor is a simply styled dining room that overlooks the atrium and a kitchen featuring a 200-year-old Dutch table and decorative Dutch wall tiles. A dark-wood paneled library on the third floor also borders the atrium and is furnished with a green silk cashmere rug, leather couch and a small bar.

The fifth floor is taken up by Pardoe's master bedroom, including a brick terrace from which you can see the old houses of Georgetown and a sliver of the Potomac.

Sam Pardoe is a prominent Washington architect and builder who actually lives here. Many of the antiques you see are family heirlooms.

Although he designed this house to suit his own tastes, he recognizes its potential for delighting others and so rents his house to small groups looking for an entertaining place to entertain.

CAPACITY

Reception: 100
Banquet: 34

LOCATION

In the Georgetown section of northwest Washington, D.C.

FOOD/BEVERAGE

WashingtonInc., the company which manages the rental of Sam Pardoe's house, handles all food and beverage arrangements and will work with you to plan your event, including your menu.

LIMITATIONS/RESTRICTIONS

The fireman's pole is off limits.

LEAD TIME FOR RESERVATIONS

Call for availability.

RATES

A flat rate of $2,100 per event.

**FACILITIES FOR THE PHYSICALLY HANDICAPPED?
YES NO SOME**
    X

SCHOONER *ALEXANDRIA*

Alexandria Seaport Foundation
1000 South Lee Street
Alexandria, Virginia 22314
703/549-7078

A tall ship with a touch of class

If you watched the parade of Tall Ships sail into New York harbor during the 1986 Statue of Liberty celebration, you know the meaning of magnificence. The Schooner *Alexandria*, which sailed with the fleet, now offers you a chance to admire her splendid lines close up.

Alexandria invites you to board her for small meetings or social events while she remains docked at the waterfront park in Old Town Alexandria. The schooner's deck measures 92 feet in length, and though you won't see them, her red sails unfurled catch more than 7,000 square feet of breeze. When you walk her old wooden decks, you get a sense of earlier days, when clipper ships ruled the waves during the great age of sail. Below deck you discover cozy captain's quarters, five double staterooms, two modern heads, a large galley and a grand, well-appointed salon. A long oak banquet table, burgundy-colored cushioned banquettes, captain's chairs and a stereo system make the salon a gracious spot for entertaining. The vessel is heated but not air-conditioned.

The Schooner *Alexandria* was built in 1929 in Sweden and sailed the Baltic as a cargo vessel until 1969. After she was remodeled for passenger use in the early 1970s, the schooner participated in several Tall Ships races. The Alexandria Seaport Foundation acquired *Alexandria* in 1983 to promote public interest in the historic seaport of Alexandria, Virginia, which was once the third largest in the country.

CAPACITY

Reception: 75 to 100 (on and below deck), 35 (below deck)
Banquet: 12 to 15 (below deck)

LOCATION

Alexandria *is docked at the Waterfront Park at the end of Prince Street in Old Town Alexandria, Virginia, which is reached from Washington via the George Washington Memorial Parkway (Washington Street within the city limits).*

FOOD/BEVERAGE

You arrange for your own caterer, although the Alexandria Seaport Foundation can recommend one if you are unfamiliar with local services. A warming stove is available in the galley.

LIMITATIONS/RESTRICTIONS

The schooner is available for early evening events and small luncheons, spring through fall. The ship is not air-conditioned.

LEAD TIME FOR RESERVATIONS

Call for availability.

RATES

$200 per hour, plus a $100 donation to the Alexandria Seaport Foundation.

FACILITIES FOR THE PHYSICALLY HANDICAPPED?
YES NO SOME
   X

THE STONE MANSION

3900 Stoneybrooke Drive
Alexandria, Virginia 22306
703/768-1777

Contemporary space in an old house

If you've grown accustomed to renting a room in a mansion for your events, or a great hall or a garden, why not rent a public park? That's what you can do at the site of the Stone Mansion.

The Stone Mansion lies on a 14-acre lot that includes woods, a playground, a picnic pavilion, tennis courts and grounds. Although this is a county park, the gates will be closed to the public if you rent the mansion and outside areas.

Of course, you can rent the mansion by itself if you want. This large 1777 dwelling is thoroughly modern inside and the first-floor rooms are for rent. There's a roomy, peach-colored entry area, a lounge featuring an 1872 rectangular grand piano, a buffet/meeting room and a kitchen. The rooms are lightly furnished for functions.

Sit-down banquets are not allowed inside the mansion, and this might be one reason why you'd want to rent the grounds. You can put up a tent on the lawn for seated dinners, although you won't be able to consume alcohol anywhere but inside the mansion.

Not much is known about the Stone Mansion's history except that Commodore Walter Brooke built it in the 18th century and settled here on his 400-acre plantation following his service in the Virginia navy.

CAPACITY

Reception: 50
Banquet: 50
Lawn party: 150
Meeting: 35 to 50

LOCATION

The Stone Mansion is five miles south of Old Town Alexandria. From the Beltway: Take Exit 2S (Telegraph Road) south to left on Parkway Street, which becomes Stoneybrooke Lane in one mile after crossing South Kings Highway. Turn left on Stoneybrooke Drive.

FOOD/BEVERAGE

You can use your own caterer or choose one from the mansion's approved list. Finger foods only are allowed and no hot foods may be prepared at the mansion. The kitchen has a refrigerator, but no oven. The mansion staff furnishes a liquor permit if you're serving alcohol.

LIMITATIONS/RESTRICTIONS

Smoking and dancing are prohibited. State law forbids consumption of alcohol outside the mansion. The mansion is available from 10:00 A.M. to 10:00 P.M., Monday through Saturday. The mansion and parking lot must be vacated by 10:00 P.M. You are responsible for cleaning up the site.

LEAD TIME FOR RESERVATIONS

Call for availability.

RATES

Mansion: $40 to $85 (total) for a minimum of four hours, plus $10 to $20 for each additional hour. Grounds: $40 to $85 for a minimum of four hours, plus $10 to $20 for each additional hour. Picnic pavilion: a flat fee of $25. Tennis courts: $10 an hour for both courts.

FACILITIES FOR THE PHYSICALLY HANDICAPPED?
YES NO SOME
   X

THE TEXTILE MUSEUM

2320 S Street, N.W.
Washington, D.C. 20008
202/667-0441

Historic houses, historic textiles

Join two mansions together, one designed by the architect of the Jefferson Memorial, John Russell Pope, and the other designed by the architect of the Woodrow Wilson House, Waddy Wood, and what do you have? The answer is the elegant structure that houses The Textile Museum. In terms of reception space, what you have are two rooms and the hall on the first floor of the Pope building, the galleries in the Waddy Wood portion of the building (only if your group numbers more than 60), plus the combined garden areas of both buildings.

From the museum's grand entrance in the Pope building you step directly into the marvelous black-and-white, marble-floored foyer. Flanking the hall at the back of the house are the Shop Gallery and the Founders Room. Each room is paneled in dark wood, has a working fireplace and great wooden furnishings that belonged to Textile Museum founder George Hewitt Myers, and opens onto the garden through French doors.

The delightful garden features a pebbled path, a fountain set in a lily pond, a large greensward behind the adjoining mansion, boxwoods, magnolias and a small, shaded pavilion.

The Textile Museum exhibits historic and handmade textiles and carpets from South America, India, China, Indonesia, Africa, Spain and the Middle East. The Pope mansion was originally the home of Myers, who founded The Textile Museum in 1925.

CAPACITY

Reception: 60 (with galleries closed); up to 125 with the galleries open

LOCATION

One block from Embassy Row (Massachusetts Avenue), 15 minutes walk from the Dupont Circle Metro station at Q Street, N.W.

FOOD/BEVERAGE

The museum must approve your caterer. A kitchen is available for warming and cooling foods.

LIMITATIONS/RESTRICTIONS

Smoking is prohibited in the museum. Music is prohibited outside the museum. The museum is available after 5:00 P.M. all year round. The museum does not allow sit-down dinners, fund raisers or wedding receptions.

LEAD TIME FOR RESERVATIONS

At least one month, but call for availability.

RATES

Reception for 60: $2,000; reception for 60 to 125: $2,500. These rates cover a four-hour period, with $250 charged for each additional quarter hour.

FACILITIES FOR THE PHYSICALLY HANDICAPPED?
YES NO SOME
X

THOMPSON BOAT CENTER

Rock Creek Parkway and Virginia Avenue, N.W.
Washington, D.C. 22002
202/333-9543

A room with a view

The view's the thing here. You can't beat it. Presented before your eyes, close-up and unobstructed, is the Potomac River, with the scenic and wooded Theodore Roosevelt Island in the background.

The Thompson Boat Center is a squat, two-story brick building hidden behind trees and bushes on a stretch of Rock Creek Parkway that runs along the Potomac. The boat center is not a marina but a storage facility for canoes and rowboats. The first floor is the storage area. Your event takes place on the second floor. This is one large, utilitarian room, not quite square or rectangular, but with its white-painted walls jutting out in odd places. You're free to decorate the room, one whole wall of which is glass, proffering you that spectacular view. This is what makes the site unique.

CAPACITY

Reception: 200
Banquet: 150 to 200

LOCATION

At the point where Rock Creek Parkway and Virginia Avenue come together, in northwest Washington, near the Watergate Apartments.

FOOD/BEVERAGE

You can arrange for your own caterer, or use the center's. This is an excellent site for a clambake prepared by specialists. Beer and wine are permitted, but not hard liquor. There is no kitchen on the premises.

LIMITATIONS/RESTRICTIONS

Live rock bands are not permitted. Events must take place after dark and may last no later than 2:00 A.M. Rowboats and canoes are available for rent from about 7:00 A.M. to dusk; there are no evening boat rentals. Consider coordinating an afternoon on the water with your evening event.

LEAD TIME FOR RESERVATIONS

At least two weeks.

RATES

A flat fee of $100 per hour.

FACILITIES FOR THE PHYSICALLY HANDICAPPED?
YES NO SOME
    X

WAKEFIELD CHAPEL

8415 Toll House Road
Annandale, Virginia 22003
703/321-7081

Church setting for secular functions

You might say that Wakefield Chapel has undergone a "born again" experience. Built in 1899, the white clapboard structure functioned as a community church until 1951, whereupon it fell into disuse for a few years. In 1979 the Fairfax County Park Authority renovated the chapel, and it has been used ever since as a meeting site for small groups.

Wakefield Chapel sits on a small rise along a residential street. The chapel is narrow and its steeple ascends higher than the building is wide. Inside, slender pine paneling covers the walls and ceiling in a diagonal pattern, giving the interior a thoroughly modern feel. Light tan wall-to-wall carpeting and recessed lighting enhance the feeling.

Although services are no longer permitted here, the chapel retains a tranquil, church-like character: the raised altar area remains, as do the arched windows and six sets of pews. Downstairs, there's a small tile-floored basement area.

CAPACITY

Meeting: 84

LOCATION

From the Beltway: Take Exit 6W (Little River Turnpike). Turn left on Wakefield Chapel Road and left again on Toll House Road. Wakefield Chapel is on the left.

FOOD/BEVERAGE

You make your own arrangements for food and beverage; alcohol is not permitted. There is no kitchen facility.

LIMITATIONS/RESTRICTIONS

Parking is available only at Chapel Square Elementary School behind the chapel. Smoking and alcohol are not permitted. The chapel is heated, but not air-conditioned. The chapel is available from 8:00 A.M. to 9:30 P.M.

LEAD TIME FOR RESERVATIONS

Up to six months ahead of time.

RATES

Minimum of four hours: $60; each additional hour: $10; refundable deposit: $100.

FACILITIES FOR THE PHYSICALLY HANDICAPPED?
YES NO SOME
X

WOODEND

8940 Jones Mill Road
Chevy Chase, Maryland 20815
301/652-9188

A stately mansion and wildlife haven

Would you like your group to escape far from the madding crowd? Take refuge in a wildlife refuge. At Woodend, you can commune with nature as well as with each other.

Woodend's stately, red-brick mansion is headquarters for the Audubon Naturalist Society, which operates the estate as a wildlife sanctuary and nature education center. Forty acres of woods, fields and thickets; 29 species of birds; and all manner of small mammals await those of you who venture on the nature trails.

If you prefer to gather indoors, the mansion's first floor rooms satisfy a variety of purposes. The Great Hall is a large and open reception area. Three sets of French doors line one wall and open to a stone patio. Exhibits of nature-oriented art are the room's main ornamentation. A small alcove under the staircase is an ideal spot for setting up a band or refreshment station.

Three smaller rooms adjoin the hall: a dining room, a meeting room that leads through French doors to a portico, and the Naturalist's Lounge. The lounge, available only for daytime rental, stands in casual contrast to the other rooms. Its dark wood paneling, booklined walls and slouching sofa carve out a comfortable spot in front of the fireplace. Glass cases display a valuable antique collection of mounted birds.

If you find yourself admiring the fine design inside and out of the Woodend mansion, there's a reason. Jefferson Memorial architect John Russell Pope designed the house in the 1920s for Captain Chester Wells, a U.S. naval officer, and his wife, an Australian heiress. The mansion and gardens copy those of Mrs. Wells's family estate in Australia.

CAPACITY

Reception: 125 inside, 150 with tent on the lawn
Banquet: 100 inside, 150 with tent
Garden party: 125, 150 with tent

LOCATION

From the Beltway: Take the Connecticut Avenue exit south toward Chevy Chase. Turn left on Manor Drive, right on Jones Bridge Road, left on Jones Mill Road.

FOOD/BEVERAGE

Woodend contracts exclusively with one caterer for food service and equipment rentals. You may make your own beverage arrangements.

LIMITATIONS/RESTRICTIONS

Smoking is prohibited in the mansion. Music and dancing are permitted inside until 11:00 P.M. Electronic amplification is not permitted outside.

LEAD TIME FOR RESERVATIONS

Call for availability. April through June and early fall are Woodend's most popular times.

RATES

$1,000 covers the use of the first floor and the grounds for a nine-hour period, including setup and cleanup time. Your date is reserved once you send a $350 deposit and a signed agreement.

FACILITIES FOR THE PHYSICALLY HANDICAPPED?
YES NO SOME
X

Sites for
200 to 500 People

AIRLIE HOUSE

Airlie Foundation
Airlie, Virginia 22186
703/347-1300
Toll free, from the Washington, D.C., area: 273-6554

An island of thought

Airlie House is a house in the same sense that Capitol Hill is a hill. You're really talking about a small community. In the case of Airlie House, you're talking about a conference community.

You have to travel a ways to get here and that's intentional. In 1959, Dr. Murdock Head founded the nonprofit educational and communication organization known as Airlie Foundation and created Airlie House. His purpose was to offer conference participants a place free from city distractions and conducive to contemplation—in other words, a veritable "island of thought," as *Life* magazine once called it.

This beautiful, 3,000 acre countryside retreat sits in the foothills of the Blue Ridge Mountains. Placed within a minute's walk of each other are pretty, yellow Georgian-style manor houses and quaint cottages that hold conference rooms, private bedrooms, a main dining room and recreational facilities for up to 250 people. The conference areas are not stodgy boardrooms but comfortably furnished rooms—often with working fireplaces—and with windows overlooking the great grounds. The rooms vary in size to accommodate your particular meeting. Each bedroom sleeps two and has its own bath.

In case you were wondering, there is indeed an Airlie House. This elegant building contains many of the conference rooms, the large banquet hall with its huge picture window, and the administrative offices. A formal garden that lies adjacent to Airlie House provides a lovely setting for a cocktail reception, with its boxwoods, seasonal plantings and gazebo.

To make sure all your needs are taken care of here, Airlie caters to a multitude of needs and interests: tennis, swimming, fishing, hiking trails, a sauna, steam room, gymnasium and other recreational facilities; the Stable Tavern for socializing; staff photographers to photograph your group, or Airlie Productions to film your conference; and audio-visual equipment and conference supplies. Airlie even has its own airstrip if you want to arrive by plane.

Newly available on the Airlie grounds is the Manor House, an elegantly furnished private home with accommodations, lounging and conference space for 20 guests. When you stay here, you dine in the center's main dining room and have access to the center's recreational facilities as well.

CAPACITY

Reception: 250
Banquet: 200
Garden party: 250
Meeting: 250
Accommodations: 240 in 120 rooms
The separate Manor House can accommodate 20 people for lodging and conferences.
There is no minimum number of people required to reserve the site.

LOCATION

From the Beltway: Take the Route 66 West exit and follow Route 66 toward Front Royal. Exit Route 66 at Gainsville, turning onto Route 29 toward Warrenton. Go about ten miles on Route 29 until you see the sign for Airlie. Turn right onto route 605 and turn left onto the Airlie grounds.

FOOD/BEVERAGE

Airlie House handles all food and beverage services, including cookouts. The menus tend toward foods that are native to

Virginia. Unless you're having a cookout or make some other special arrangement, you eat all three meals in the main dining room.

LIMITATIONS/RESTRICTIONS

Children and pets are not allowed.

LEAD TIME FOR RESERVATIONS

Eight to 12 months.

RATES

Overnight stays: $65 per person for doubles, $81 per person for singles. These rates include lodging, three meals, two coffee breaks and use of the conference facilities.
Day guests: $14 for lunch, $31 for lunch and dinner. These rates cover charges for coffee breaks and the use of the conference facilities, as well as the meals.
The Manor House: $70 for doubles, $100 for singles, plus a $500 per day exclusive-use charge.
Rates may increase slightly in 1989.

FACILITIES FOR THE PHYSICALLY HANDICAPPED?
YES NO SOME
       X

THE ARTS CLUB OF WASHINGTON

2017 Eye Street, N.W.
Washington, D.C. 20006
202/331-7282

A city site with surprising features

So maybe you think your organization is asking for the moon. You say they want to hold their function at a historic home in downtown Washington, one that has a garden and a ballroom, plenty of art and atmosphere? Consider the Arts Club of Washington (illustrated on the cover).

Located just a few blocks from both the White House and Georgetown, the club occupies two connecting 19th-century townhouses. Sure enough, there's a ballroom and it has a stage, piano and great wooden doors opening to the street. Also on the main floor are two elegant banquet rooms furnished with antiques and Waterford-crystal chandeliers. French doors in the back banquet room lead to a beautiful, tree-shaded patio surrounded by a sculpture garden. This space is surprisingly large and private.

The cozy library and cheerful drawing rooms on the second floor are pleasant places to call a meeting to order or to take tea and make conversation. There's also an informal meeting place in the dark and mysterious basement, which is equipped with a set-up bar (minus the liquor) and ice cream parlor chairs and tables.

There are several reasons you'll want to explore all these rooms. First of all, the entire property is an art gallery featuring the work of Washington artists. Second, the site is historic. James Monroe lived here in 1817 while he waited for the White House to be renovated following its partial destruction during the War of 1812.

Finally, it's fun. The way the two houses merge is charming. Just when you think you've seen it all you come upon an unnoticed set of stairs that leads to still another level, or a door that leads to a balcony, or a hall that leads to who knows where. The Arts Club is a wonderful place to wander.

CAPACITY

Reception: 300
Banquet: 125
Garden party: 300
Meeting: 5 to 125

LOCATION

Just off Pennsylvania Avenue in downtown Washington, a few blocks west of the White House and east of Georgetown. You can park on the street or in nearby parking garages.

FOOD/BEVERAGE

The Arts Club caters all functions and will work with you to plan the meal. You provide the alcohol.

LIMITATIONS/RESTRICTIONS

Music must end by midnight.

LEAD TIME FOR RESERVATIONS

Four to six months for weekend functions and one month for functions that will take place during the week.

RATES

$250 to $1,000 (considered a donation to the club, not a fee), depending upon the number of rooms you reserve.

FACILITIES FOR THE PHYSICALLY HANDICAPPED?
YES NO SOME
   X

THE ATHENAEUM

201 Prince Street

Alexandria, Virginia 22314

703/548-0035

A simply grand old hall and garden

It's the grandness that grabs you at the Athenaeum. In a neighborhood of narrow brick townhouses, the Athenaeum dominates with its Greek Revival architecture, majestic columns and porticoed entrance.

The grandest part of all is the hall itself. The carpenters raised high the roof beams when they built this structure in 1851 and then they topped the main room with a coved ceiling. The hall is large and unfurnished, the walls stretch tall and white, and the windows are many and oversized. Overall, the effect is one of space and light.

In addition to the great hall and its smaller adjoining room, you also have use of the tiny patio and sculpture garden enclosed by a high brick wall in back. If you're interested in exploring historic Old Town while you're here, follow the path that leads from the garden back out to Prince Street. You'll be charmed to find that not only buildings have been preserved, but some of the streets as well. For example, the portion of Prince Street that runs from the Athenaeum to the waterfront is still cobblestone.

When the Athenaeum is not hosting a function, it serves as an art gallery for the Northern Virginia Fine Arts Association, which has its headquarters here. If the Athenaeum strikes you as the perfect setting for gala events and art exhibits, you may be surprised to learn of the other uses the building has had—first as a bank, then as a commissary, a church and later as a medicine warehouse. There are some good stories associated with the building's history. Ask the staff person at your function what happened to the bank customers' money during the Civil War.

CAPACITY

Reception: 175 inside, 225 when both the hall and garden are used
Banquet: 72 inside, 100 when both the hall and garden are used
Garden party: 75
Meeting: 100

LOCATION

In Old Town Alexandria, one street south of King Street and two blocks from the Potomac waterfront.

FOOD/BEVERAGE

You're free to choose your own caterer and tent vendor, although the Athenaeum has a list available. A small kitchen on the bottom floor of the building may be used to warm and cool foods.

LIMITATIONS/RESTRICTIONS

The Athenaeum allows only medium-level amplified music, and the music must end by 11:00 P.M. weeknights and by midnight on weekends. Cleanup must be completed no later than one hour after the event has ended. The Athenaeum usually rents its facility during late spring, summer, early autumn and during the Christmas season.

LEAD TIME FOR RESERVATIONS

Call for availability.

RATES

$100 per hour, with a two-hour minimum. The Athenaeum charges you for setup and cleanup time and requires you to pay a $200 nonrefundable security deposit, which the facility applies to your total rental fee.

FACILITIES FOR THE PHYSICALLY HANDICAPPED?
YES NO SOME
   X

THE BARNS OF WOLF TRAP

1635 Trap Road
Vienna, Virginia 22180
703/938-8463

Old World cum New World

If you think about it, you realize that a barn just happens to meet many of the essentials required for a successful event; it's usually roomy, it's got atmosphere and you can use it for a variety of purposes. Yeah, you say, but isn't it a little primitive?

Not these barns. There are two of them, the German Barn, dating from 1725, and the English Barn, dating from 1770. Both barns are from farms in New York State, which were dismantled and reconstructed at Wolf Trap in 1981. The rebuilding process involved 18th-century techniques and the barns were rebuilt inside out, so that the interior presents you with weathered boarding, hand-cut timbers, polished pine floors and a pleasant reminder of days gone by.

But just as care has been taken to preserve the beauty of these structures, care has been taken to incorporate modern features for your total convenience. The German barn is also a theatre and has a fully equipped stage, sophisticated lighting and sound systems, and a balcony with fixed seating. The adjoining English Barn is a little smaller and features a fully equipped, beam-enclosed bar. A lobby next to the English barn provides additional space.

You can rent one or both barns for any sort of function, from presentations to cocktail parties to black tie affairs. Included in the rental of either barn is the use of an inner brick courtyard, which abuts both barns.

Down the road from The Barns is the Wolf Trap Filene Center, Washington's summer showplace for concerts, ballet, opera and other performances. The Filene Center is an outdoor amphitheater surrounded by rolling hills and trees. If you're booking The Barns for business, why not check out the Filene Center's schedule, which runs from late May to early September? You might find that Emmylou Harris, the Alvin Ailey Dance Theater or perhaps the National Symphony Orchestra is performing the same day you've rented the Barns. If your group wants to attend the show after wrapping up business, contact Group Sales (see section entitled "How to Book Group Seating for Theater Performances"). Consider purchasing lawn tickets rather than the pavilion seats. That way, you can pack a picnic, including champagne, and savor the experience in true Washington fashion.

CAPACITY

Reception: 400
Banquet: 225
Meeting: 350

LOCATION

From either the Beltway or Route 66: Take Route 7 West four miles to left on Towlston Road; go 2½ miles to The Barns on the left. The Barns are located 12 miles from Dulles Airport and only a few minutes from Tysons Corner.

FOOD/BEVERAGE

You can hire your own caterer or choose one from Wolf Trap's approved list. Wolf Trap furnishes all alcohol and bartenders. The site includes a prep kitchen.

LIMITATIONS/RESTRICTIONS

Smoking is prohibited in the German Barn.

LEAD TIME FOR RESERVATIONS

The Barns are available year-round, subject to Wolf Trap's performance schedule. May, June, September and October are the most popular months and weekday events are easiest to reserve. Allow at least nine months for spring weekend affairs and three months for events throughout the rest of the year.

RATES

Meetings: $75 to $150 per hour. Parties: $675 to $1,225 (total), with a six-hour minimum. The cost varies depending upon the choice and the number of barns you rent. Overtime charges run from $125 per hour for the use of both barns and $90 per hour for the use of one barn.

FACILITIES FOR THE PHYSICALLY HANDICAPPED?
YES NO SOME
X

CAPITOL HILL CLUB

300 First Street, S.E.
Washington, D.C. 20003
202/484-4590

Republicans' hangout on the Hill

You'd never guess that John Wayne and Winston Churchill had anything in common, but they both were once members of the Capitol Hill Club. So were Dwight D. Eisenhower, Spiro T. Agnew and cowboy star Gene Autry. In fact, the 36-year-old club welcomes as a member anyone who has dealings on the Hill. To rent the club for an event, you must be a member or be sponsored by one.

Nine rooms are available for events, and whether your group numbers 15 for lunch or 400 for a reception, there is a space just suited to your size and type of event. Each room is tastefully decorated in subdued colors, mostly creams and blue-greens, and furnishings recall colonial Williamsburg. Portraits of Republican presidents hang on the walls throughout the club.

If you're planning a reception for 200 or so, you'd probably want to rent the lovely Eisenhower Lounge on the lobby level. The comfortable furniture is arranged in cozy clusters around the room, making it easy for a large crowd to mingle and still carry on private conversations. A display case at one end shows off an impressive collection of decorative elephants.

The Presidential Dining Room is a handsome banquet area with its many long windows hung with handsome teal curtains. This room also hides a surprise: Underneath the carpet lies a dance floor. The room accommodates 225 seated, without the dance floor, and 160 seated, with the dance floor.

Other rooms include one large and light-filled banquet/ reception area that can be partitioned into four separate chambers; two formal but intimate conference rooms; and a small, casual meeting room whose walls are hung with framed political cartoons.

(Democrats, you've got your own hangout—see the National Democratic Club listing.)

CAPACITY

Reception: 400
Banquet: 240
Meeting: 240

LOCATION

On Capitol Hill, directly across from the Capitol South Metro station.

FOOD/BEVERAGE

The club prepares all the food for your event but will work with you to plan your menu. The club also handles all beverage arrangements.

LIMITATIONS/RESTRICTIONS

To hold an event here you must either belong to the club or be sponsored by a member.

LEAD TIME FOR RESERVATIONS

Depends on the type of event you're planning and the number of attendees; call for availability.

RATES

Meal charges range from $15 per person for weekday events to $30 per person for weekend events, plus gratuity and tax. On the weekends, there is a $30 per person minimum for food and beverage and a 100 person minimum required to reserve the club. In addition, there is a $30 bartender fee per bar setup. Room rates are as follows: Private rooms used for meetings without meals—$100, regardless of the length of the meeting; private rooms used for meals with fewer than 25 persons—$25, plus a $30 waiter fee; the Bolton Room and the Governor's suite (the most formal meeting areas)—$75 each; the Presidential Dining Room—$500, when used on the weekend. The Presidential Dining Room is not available for rentals during the week.

FACILITIES FOR THE PHYSICALLY HANDICAPPED?
YES NO SOME
X

CARNEGIE LIBRARY

University of the District of Columbia
800 Mount Vernon Place, N.W.
Washington, D.C. 20001
202/282-2057
Mailing address: University of the District of
Columbia
Office of Special Events
4200 Connecticut Avenue, N.W.
Washington, D.C. 20008

Beautiful building, convenient location

As you head toward the D.C. Convention Center or make
your way to one of the new hotels in that vicinity, you
might catch sight of a stately, older building standing alone
on its own grass island, apart from its modern, downtown
neighbors. This is Carnegie Library, once part of Washington's public library system, and now owned by the University of the District of Columbia.

Upon entering this early 20th-century Beaux Arts building, you pass through a small foyer into a grand interior
hall. Here you can hold receptions, banquets and dances
under a skylight roof. A marble floor, Palladian windows
and a swirling double staircase give this open, unfurnished
space a classically elegant feel while modern art and track
lighting bestow contemporary touches. Should you happen
to glance up, you'll see the names of Shakespeare, Bacon,
Newton, Plato, Homer and Galileo engraved at the top of
the central columns.

Downstairs lies the other space available for rent—the
community room. This is a good place to hold meetings.
Wall-to-wall carpeting is a burnt sienna color and the walls
are white. The room is dividable into four parts by parti-
tions.

117

CAPACITY

Reception: 400 (hall)
Banquet: 200 (hall)
Meeting: 150

LOCATION

*Catty-corner from the D.C. Convention Center in downtown
Washington.*

FOOD/BEVERAGE

*You can choose any caterer that is licensed in Washington, D.C.
To serve or sell alcohol requires a liquor permit from the D.C.
Alcohol Beverage Control board, but the university will handle
this for you.*

LIMITATIONS/RESTRICTIONS

*The hall is available after 6:00 P.M. any day, and the community
room is available 8:00 A.M. to 10:00 P.M. Monday through
Friday and 9:00 A.M. to 1:00 P.M., Saturdays. (You can use the
community room at other times on the weekend, but only by
special arrangement and at additional cost.)*

LEAD TIME FOR RESERVATIONS

Call for availability.

RATES

*Hall: $1,571.83 for a minimum of four hours; community room:
$64.42 for a minimum of four hours on the weekend and
holidays, and no charge during the week. For functions lasting
over four hours, there is an overtime charge of approximately
$150 per hour. If you charge people a fee to attend a function
held during the week in the community room, the university
will charge you its standard weekend fee.*

FACILITIES FOR THE PHYSICALLY HANDICAPPED?
YES NO SOME
     X

The first floor of the library is accessible to the handicapped.

THE CHERRY BLOSSOM

Potomac Riverboat Company
205 The Strand
Alexandria, Virginia 22314
703/684-0580

Rollin' on the river

Even before you step aboard *The Cherry Blossom* you recognize that this is no ordinary boat. If, as you stand admiring it, the movie *Showboat* comes to mind, it's because the 1984-built *Cherry Blossom* was modeled after those 19th century paddlewheelers that brought entertainment to ports along America's rivers. The three-deck vessel is painted white, the huge paddlewheel is painted yellow and a wrought-iron, mahogany-topped rail runs around the outside decks. The captain sits inside his pilot's house perch ready to take you rollin' on the river.

The Cherry Blossom was designed specifically for elegant, privately chartered entertaining; nevertheless, the features you find within may surprise you: mahogany paneling, brass fixtures, artfully etched windows, gold and red painted tin ceilings, plush wall-to-wall carpeting, scalloped gold and pale green wallpaper and grand chandeliers. The two enclosed lower decks are equipped with air conditioning and heating, so *The Cherry Blossom* is ready to roll anytime you are during the year.

You can hold any sort of event on board, from a dance to a fancy dinner. All the while, *The Cherry Blossom* slowly showboats its way along the Potomac, passing the Washington monuments if you go north, or the quaint sights of Old Town Alexandria and Mount Vernon if you go south. You can stay inside and see it all from the boat's many windows; or venture out to the promenade deck that encircles the enclosed second level or to the open, third-level Hurricane Deck. For the best view of all, go up top with the captain.

CAPACITY

Reception: 400
Banquet: 200
Meeting: 200

LOCATION

You board The Cherry Blossom *at her home port in Old Town Alexandria, right behind the Torpedo Factory at the foot of Cameron Street.*

FOOD/BEVERAGE

The Cherry Blossom *has an approved list of caterers from which you must choose. The boat's galley is fully equipped for cooking and cooling. There are also ice machines on board.*

LIMITATIONS/RESTRICTIONS

No specific restrictions.

LEAD TIME FOR RESERVATIONS

A year for spring and weekend events; three to four months otherwise.

RATES

Peak season (April through October): evenings and weekends- $35 per person with a minimum charge of $3,500 for a three-hour cruise. Additional hours may be purchased for $5 per person, with a minimum charge of $800. Weekdays between 8:00 A.M. and 4:00 P.M.: $15 per person with a minimum charge of $1,000 for a two-hour cruise.

Off-season (November through March): evenings and weekends—$27 per person, with a minimum of $2,700 for a three-hour cruise. Off-season weekday rates are the same as peak season weekday rates. These rates include exclusive use of the boat plus beverages at the premium brand bar, among other things. The Cherry Blossom is also available for luncheon packages, dockside meetings and seminars.

FACILITIES FOR THE PHYSICALLY HANDICAPPED?
YES NO SOME
    X

CONFEDERATE MEMORIAL HALL

1322 Vermont Avenue, N.W.

Washington, D.C. 20005

202/483-5700

Washington's embassy for the South

It may strike you as odd that Washington, D.C., the capital city for the Union, should have a shrine honoring the Confederacy. The Confederate Memorial Association, which owns the Confederate Memorial Hall, takes its mission seriously all the same. After the Civil War, the mansion was used as a Confederate veterans' home and, since 1919, the Association has used it as a meeting place, library and museum.

The Confederate Memorial Hall is a four-story brownstone whose spacious first floor is available for meetings, dinners and receptions. What were once three separate rooms have been joined to make one spacious area that extends from the three-sided front bay window to the kitchen at the back of the house.

In between, you'll find ornamental oak-paneled fireplaces with large mirrors hanging over their mantels, chandeliers and hardwood floors. War Between the States memorabilia abound. There are hundred-year-old oil portraits of Confederate Generals Robert E. Lee, Stonewall Jackson, Fitzhugh Lee and others. Bookcases contain works about the South and the war. There's even a framed bail bond for Jefferson Davis, who, you remember, was the president of the Confederacy.

When you hold an event here, Southern ladies in antebellum gowns and Confederate Embassy Guards in full uniform attend you. You can expect your meal to have a Confederate taste to it, too—the hall serves country ham, sweet potato pie and other strictly Southern foods. The Confederate Embassy Band can also provide period music played on period instruments.

CAPACITY

Reception: 150 (inside), 250 (inside and tented lot outside)
Banquet: 75
Meeting: 75 to 100

LOCATION

*In northwest Washington, two blocks north of Massachusetts
Avenue and eight blocks from the White House.*

FOOD/BEVERAGE

*You can choose your own caterer or arrange for the Hall to cater
your function, but the Hall serves only Southern food.*

LEAD TIME FOR RESERVATIONS

Call for availability.

RATES

*A basic fee of $100 per hour. Costumed personnel, music and
catering fees are quoted separately.*

FACILITIES FOR THE PHYSICALLY HANDICAPPED?
YES NO SOME
           X

DECATUR CARRIAGE HOUSE

1610 H Street, N.W
Washington, D.C. 20006
202/673-4273

History and style carry the event

The Decatur Carriage House is that rare thing: a newly constructed, thoroughly modern and spacious meeting facility on the site of a historic home. By holding an event here, you can tour a marvelous Washington landmark that's been the home of a vice president, congressmen and famous others, yet you avoid the usual historic property restrictions regarding food, drink, size and entertainment.

Situated on the same spot where War of 1812 naval hero Stephen Decatur once stabled his horses, the carriage house offers you one large hall for meetings, receptions and banquets. You enter the hall through an octagonal-shaped foyer, the floor design of which represents a mariner's compass.

An exceptionally pleasing color scheme greets you inside the hall: the walls are pale yellow and white and the carpet is a deep royal blue bedecked with gold stars. Exceptional, too, are the room's dimensions. The hall covers 2,100 square feet and has a vaulted ceiling. Floor-to-ceiling windows overlook, and French doors lead to, the private garden and brick-paved courtyard. The beautiful garden is floodlit at night and is available only with rental of the carriage house.

Opposite the carriage house is the Decatur House Museum. Ground floor rooms reflect Federal-period decorating and life-styles. There's a bedroom on this floor, for example, as there was when Decatur lived here, and the Sheraton chairs and Chippendale table you see in the room are original to the Decatur family.

Upstairs rooms reflect the Victorian period and appear as they were when the Beales, a prominent California family, inhabited the house, from the 1870s to 1956. A magnificent American Centennial glass chandelier hangs in the south drawing room, the ceilings are painted with foliate designs, and an elaborate parquet floor in the north drawing room features an inlaid California state seal. You can arrange to tour the Decatur House Museum for an additional fee when you rent the carriage house.

CAPACITY

Reception: 250 (carriage house), 500 (carriage house and tented garden)
Banquet: 120 (carriage house), 250 (carriage house and tented garden)
Garden party: 500
Meeting: 90, seated theater-style

LOCATION

Across from Lafayette Square and two blocks from the White House; within walking distance of the Farragut West and Farragut North Metro stations.

FOOD/BEVERAGE

The Decatur Carriage House requires you to choose a caterer

from their approved list. There is a kitchen available equipped with a refrigerator/freezer and electric outlets.

LIMITATIONS/RESTRICTIONS

The use of a tent in the garden is mandatory if the number of attendees exceeds the capacity of the interior of the carriage house. Dancing and amplified music are prohibited after 11:30 P.M. in the garden. Decatur House has no parking facility; however, you can arrange to have valet parking or reserve parking garages in the area. Politically sponsored events are not allowed.

LEAD TIME FOR RESERVATIONS

Like most of Washington, the Decatur Carriage House is busiest from mid-September to mid-December and from March to June. The staff recommends that you call for availability.

RATES

For four hours' use: carriage house—$1,500; carriage house and tented garden—$2,000; carriage house, garden and tour of Decatur House Museum—$2,500. Additional time: $100 for one hour, $200 for two hours and $400 for three hours. The garden, by itself, is not available for rent. Rates may increase in 1988.

FACILITIES FOR THE PHYSICALLY HANDICAPPED?
YES NO SOME
X

FOLGER SHAKESPEARE LIBRARY

201 East Capitol Street, S.E.
Washington, D.C. 20003
202/544-4600

"Go to the feast, revel and domineer"

Gather at the Folger Shakespeare Library and watch as the Falstaffs, Prince Hals, Rosalinds and Cleopatras among you are revealed. In this Tudor "great house" setting, a meeting can provide high drama, a banquet may seem a royal feast, a standup reception is a merry mingling of actors removing their masks.

Each of the five rooms available is spectacular. As you proceed apace through the Elizabethan Great Hall or into the adjoining Old Reading Room, you'll fancy yourselves in a castle. The two rooms are representative of Tudor banquet halls; each measures about 127 feet long and sports a towering ceiling. Standup receptions take place in the reading room where Shakespeare's spirit is in beautiful evidence—stained glass windows depict the Seven Ages of Man described in *As You Like It*. The Great Hall is the library's main banquet area and a handsome one at that with its patterned tile floor and blocked wall paneling.

You see more stained glass, displaying characters from Shakespeare's plays, in the Founders' Room, a space suitable for small meetings and receptions. This is a paneled Tudor-style room furnished with high-backed chairs and a 17th-century refectory table. The New Reading Room is also available to Great Hall/Old Reading Room users for an additional fee. Another small room, the extremely elegant Board Room, is available for intimate dinners. Donors of $15,000 or more may have seated dinner in the Old Reading Room, with special permission of the Director.

When the Shakespeare Theatre Company is not staging a play, you can even reserve this space for an event. The theater suggests an Elizabethan public playhouse, only it's fully enclosed.

CAPACITY

Reception: 750 (Great Hall and Reading Rooms)
Banquet: 180
Theatre event: 250
Meeting: (Founders' Room, 25; Board Room, 20–60; other rooms, 250
Dinner in Board Room: 60

LOCATION

One block east of the U.S. Capitol Building.

FOOD/BEVERAGE

The Library prefers that you use a caterer from its approved list. A warming kitchen is available, as well as a service elevator.

LIMITATIONS/RESTRICTIONS

Use of the Folger Shakespeare Library is limited to corporate donors who have paid a minimum, unrestricted cash contribution of $2,500. Political fundraisers are not allowed. Loud music is not allowed in the Great Hall when there are performances going on in the Theatre. Banquets are permitted only in the Great Hall. Use of the Old Reading Room is available only to corporate donors who contribute $10,000 or more to the Library.

LEAD TIME FOR RESERVATIONS

At least six months, and nine months for December events, but call for availability.

RATES

Membership fee: unrestricted cash contributions of $2,500 or more to the Library. Tax-exempt educational and cultural organizations with IRS 501(c)3 documentation may receive a 25 percent discount. Rental fees: Great Hall-$4,000; Theatre—$2,000; Great Hall/Reading Room package—$7,500; Great Hall/Theatre package—$5,000; Great Hall/Theatre/Reading Room package—$8,500; Founders' Room—$500; Reading Room—$7,500; Board Room—$1,000.

FACILITIES FOR THE PHYSICALLY HANDICAPPED?
YES NO SOME
X

GREAT FALLS GRANGE AND SCHOOLHOUSE

9818 Georgetown Pike

Great Falls, Virginia 22066

Mailing address: P.O. Box 307

Great Falls, Virginia 22066

703/759-6037

Multi-purpose space in a park

There are no hidden treasures here. What you see is what you get. If your main requirement is plenty of space, read on.

The Grange is a 1929, two-story, red-brick building with a long set of concrete steps leading up from either side to the main entrance. Inside are two large halls. The upstairs hall is plain, but pleasing with its high, vaulted wood ceiling and hardwood floor. Six windows line each side wall, letting in lots of light during the day. At night, dangling brass chandeliers and fan lights illuminate the place. (There is no air conditioning.) A large raised stage at one end of the room makes a great bandstand or showplace for theater productions and presentations. The basement hall is just as roomy but lacks ornamentation, with a tile floor and painted steel columns.

Next door to the Grange is a white frame schoolhouse that dates from 1890. This building has been completely renovated so it really doesn't show its age. There are two bare rooms inside with hardwood floors and globe fan lights.

Both the Grange and the schoolhouse lie in a small park setting that includes a picnic pavilion and playground. The Grange, the schoolhouse and the pavilion are each available separately for rental.

CAPACITY

Reception: 300 (Grange), 50 (schoolhouse)
Banquet: 105 (Grange), 30 (schoolhouse)
Picnic: 200
Meeting/Performances: 200 (Grange)

LOCATION

From the Beltway: Take Exit 13 (Georgetown Pike, Route 193) west and go six miles to park entrance on the right.

FOOD/BEVERAGE

You arrange your own catering and beverage service. A liquor permit is required if you're going to serve alcohol.

LIMITATIONS/RESTRICTIONS

Smoking is prohibited. You may not use nails, tacks or tape to hang decorations.

LEAD TIME FOR RESERVATIONS

Call for availability.

RATES

Rates vary according to the space rented, the type of function and type of organization: from $70 for a Fairfax County nonprofit organization's four-hour social affair in the Grange to $295 for the rental of the Grange, schoolhouse and picnic pavilion by a noncounty profit organization for a four-hour event.

FACILITIES FOR THE PHYSICALLY HANDICAPPED?
YES NO SOME
    X

GREEN SPRING FARM

4601 Green Spring Road
Alexandria, Virginia 22312
703/941-6066

Colonial farm raises contemporary art

Steep yourselves in history, garden greenery and art—
they're all here at Green Spring Farm. Built in 1760 by
gentleman farmer John Moss, the brick farmhouse has
served over the years as a meeting place for all sorts of
people. Virginia Methodists held church services here in its
early years, Civil War soldiers visited the farm in the 1860s,
and writers Saul Bellow, Aldous Huxley and Dylan Thomas
are a few of the famous guests who have gathered here in
the 20th century.

Green Spring Farm sits on secluded park grounds that
include a semicircular boxwood hedge, an herb garden, seasonal plantings and two huge black walnut trees. You can
reserve this beautifully landscaped area by itself or in conjunction with the rental of the house. The three-story farmhouse contains an art gallery on its first floor, the only floor
available for rent. Along the 17th-century paneled and
white-painted walls, local artists display original works
ranging from quilts to prints. Fireplaces and floor-to-ceiling
windows complete this quaint picture.

CAPACITY

Reception: 60 (inside)
Banquet: 35 to 40 (total seated in both rooms)
Garden party: 300
Business breakfast or meeting: 60

LOCATION

*From the Beltway: Take Exit 6E (Little River Turnpike). Go
three miles east to left on Green Spring Road to the park
entrance.*

FOOD/BEVERAGE

You can choose your own caterer. A kitchen is available for warming and cooling foods, but not for cooking.

LIMITATIONS/RESTRICTIONS

Smoking is prohibited in the house. A liquor permit is required if you plan to serve alcohol. If the number of your party exceeds the 60-person limit of the house, the staff strongly recommends that you rent a tent. Green Spring Farm is available Saturday, from 9:00 A.M. to midnight and Sunday through Friday, from 8:00 A.M. to noon and from 4:00 P.M. to midnight.

LEAD TIME FOR RESERVATIONS

At least three weeks, but the staff will accept reservations 12 months in advance.

RATES

House: $200; grounds: $150; house and grounds: $350. Each of these rates is for a minimum period of four hours. An event running over four hours incurs a $50 per hour charge. A $150 security deposit is required to rent Green Spring Farm, but this is returned to you after the event, minus a $35 cleaning fee, assuming the site has not been damaged.

FACILITIES FOR THE PHYSICALLY HANDICAPPED?
YES NO SOME
   X

JEFFERSON AUDITORIUM

Department of Agriculture Building
14th and Independence Avenue, S.W.
Washington, D.C. 20250
202/447-2911

A burst of color in a government building

Like many government buildings, the Department of Agriculture's South Building is long and gray and labyrinthian in layout. Within this sprawling structure, however, lies a surprisingly handsome auditorium.

In keeping with the size of the building, the Jefferson Auditorium is large, seating 480 people. Great flourishes of three-dimensional blue, green and yellow flower petals decorate the 30-foot-high ceiling. The walls are painted blue at the top, paneled in the middle and set in green marble at the bottom. Very comfortable rose-cushioned seats and a deep blue carpet complete this colorful picture.

Any meeting, lecture or performance you schedule here will get a thoroughly professional treatment. The auditorium features a sizeable stage, dressing rooms, stage lighting, sound system, projection booth and podium.

CAPACITY

Meeting/lecture/performance: 480

LOCATION

Within walking distance of the Mall, at the corner of 14th Street and Independence Avenue, S.W.

FOOD/BEVERAGE

Food and beverages are not allowed inside the auditorium. There is a large cafeteria in the building that's open during the week from 7:00 A.M. to 3:30 P.M. Your other choice is to go the mile

133

or so up to Capitol Hill where there are many bars and restaurants.

LIMITATIONS/RESTRICTIONS

Smoking, food and beverages are prohibited.

LEAD TIME FOR RESERVATIONS

One month.

RATES

October through March: $120 per hour, from 6:00 A.M. to 6:00 P.M., and $127.50 per hour after 6:00 P.M. April through September: $103 per hour from 6:00 A.M. to 6:00 P.M., and $110.50 per hour after 6:00 P.M. Additional charges include $20 an hour for a production assistant during regular hours and $30 an hour for overtime.

FACILITIES FOR THE PHYSICALLY HANDICAPPED?
YES NO SOME
X

McLEAN GARDENS BALLROOM

3811 Porter Street, N.W.
Washington, D.C. 20016
301/585-9277

A belle of a ballroom

When you enter the McLean Gardens Ballroom, you can feel time slow down and the annoyances of the outside world disappear. Life is warm and wonderful and everyone in it is a gracious and exceptional human being.

How does the ballroom create this atmosphere? Maybe it's the epic dimensions of the room: 54 by 45 feet, with a 40-foot-high ceiling. Maybe it's the pale, pale yellow of the walls. Maybe it's the tasteful arrangement of Williamsburg-style furnishings. At any rate, this one-room site is at once intimate and elegant.

The ballroom was built in the 1940s as a recreation center for soldiers. In 1984, the ballroom was completely renovated. Four huge white pillars define the room, setting off the center parquet dance floor from the living room setups on either side. Elaborate moldings, working fireplaces at either end, chandeliers and great swags of green and gold drapes at the long windows are some of the room's finishing touches.

Not to worry—you don't have to dance to hold a function here. The ballroom is available not only for dances, but for receptions, dinners and meetings.

CAPACITY

Reception: 350
Banquet: 110, seated with a buffet; 140, seated without a buffet
Meeting: 150 to 175

LOCATION

One block off of Wisconsin Avenue, N.W., within walking distance of the Washington National Cathedral.

FOOD/BEVERAGE

You can choose any caterer who meets the ballroom's insurance requirements. A service kitchen and preparation room are available.

LEAD TIME FOR RESERVATIONS

Call for availability.

LIMITATIONS/RESTRICTIONS

No specific limitations; discuss your requests with management.

RATES

$1,775 for an eight-hour period. Tables and chairs included, also special event planning services.

FACILITIES FOR THE PHYSICALLY HANDICAPPED?
YES NO SOME
X

MERIDIAN HOUSE INTERNATIONAL

1630 Crescent Place, N.W.
Washington, D.C. 20009
202/667-6800

A thoroughly French grand mansion

As the French might say, Meridian House, *c'est une maison magnifique!* You think of France when you see Meridian House for several reasons. It sits on a shady street behind a high stone wall, an imposing limestone structure designed in the style of an 18th-century estate found in the Ile de France. French antique furniture, marble bust sculpture, brass hardware and lighting fixtures, and lattice parquetry floors are some of its interior features. Even the garden's 42 linden trees were imported from France.

You can rent the main floor's reception gallery, loggia, library, drawing room and dining room; the rear and side gardens, in season; and a conference room on the lower level. The gallery, loggia and garden are all in a line down the center of the mansion, forming a natural reception area. Waterford-crystal torchieres, large blue Chinese temple jars and mirrored walls distinguish the gallery. The loggia is a spacious and rounded sun room with long arching windows that frame views of the lovely linden trees and pebbled courtyard.

The library and drawing room adjoin the center areas, expanding available reception space in a delightful way. The library is an unusual jade green color and has built-in book-shelves and map cases. Next door, the drawing room features an antique Persian Kerman carpet, a 19th-century Steinway and pale yellow walls.

On the other side of the house is the dining room, ideal for banquets and buffets. A beautiful English tapestry hangs on one wall; its dimensions determined the size of this room and the height of ceilings throughout the house.

The board room on the lower level can accommodate small meetings—up to 25 around the table.

Scheduled for opening in late 1988 is the adjacent White-Meyer House, recently purchased by Meridian House and now under renovation. The magnificent Georgian-style mansion was also designed by Meridian House architect John Russell Pope. Rented together, the two mansions will offer double Meridian House's current capacity for meetings and events.

CAPACITY

Reception: 500
Banquet: 90 to 100
Garden party: 500 to 800
Meeting: 10 to 100, in one room

LOCATION

Straight out 16th Street, N.W., about 1¼ miles from the White House.

FOOD/BEVERAGE

You must choose a caterer from the MHI-approved list. There is a pantry on the main floor available for warming and cooling foods, but not cooking.

LIMITATIONS/RESTRICTIONS

Red wine and dancing are prohibited. Smoking is restricted to certain areas. Fundraising is not allowed. Use of Meridian

House for events is restricted to corporate benefactors and to nonprofit organizations whose goals are complementary to those of Meridian House—that is, aimed at promoting international understanding.

LEAD TIME FOR RESERVATIONS

At least three weeks, but call for availability.

RATES

From $400, for one room, to $2,000, for use of all the rental areas. Rates vary, too, depending upon whether you are a corporate member, benefactor, or a nonprofit organization. Corporate members and benefactors are required to make a donation to Meridian House. There are additional fees for security and other services. Fees are subject to change without notice.

FACILITIES FOR THE PHYSICALLY HANDICAPPED?
YES NO SOME
   X

Meridian House has a street-level back entrance and an elevator that will take you to the main floor.

MOUNT AIRY PLANTATION

Box 1008, Rosaryville Road
Upper Marlboro, Maryland 20772
301-856-1860

Maryland hunt country's historic estate

Maryland's founding family, the Calverts, hunted here. George and Martha Washington slept here. Eleanor Washington, their daughter, married here. Presidents Taft, Wilson, Coolidge, Hoover and Roosevelt were all, at various times, entertained here. And now it's your turn.

Up a winding dirt road you go until you come upon this marvelous, restored mansion poised on a summit set in the woods. You can reserve the whole house and grounds, if you want, or just one of the seven rooms. There are even two suites available for overnight stays.

The house's architecture is a little bit of this and a little bit of that: English cottage, Federal, Georgian and Greek Revival styles. Somehow, the designs blend together inside to create warm and inviting places for meetings, receptions and dinners.

The dark-stained pine-paneled Hunt Room is comfortable and cozy. Adjoining the Hunt Room is a chamber that dates to 1725, making it the oldest standing portion of the building. The Lord Baltimore Lounge, as it is called, is decorated in red floral-patterned curtains, rugs and upholstery. A huge hearth dominates one wall and a smaller working fireplace is set in the opposite wall.

There are five light-filled dining rooms, two upstairs and three down. Each is a pleasant ensemble of colonial hues, flowered carpeting and attractive table settings. Of the five, the main dining room is the prettiest. The sky is the ceiling in this glass-topped room, and an entire wall of tall French doors overlooks the estate's back lawn. Venture outdoors and you'll see more—a parterre, a greenhouse, crab apple and white oak trees, boxwoods, holly bushes and azaleas.

CAPACITY

Reception: 200 (throughout the house)
Banquet: 200 (throughout the house)
Garden party: 250
Meeting: from 30 to 80 in a single room

LOCATION

*From the Beltway: Take Exit 11A and go south on Route 4
about four miles to Route 223. Turn right on Route 223
(Woodyard Road) and go about two miles to Rosaryville Road.
Take a left and follow the mile-long dirt road to the top.*

FOOD/BEVERAGE

*Mount Airy Plantation is a restaurant as well as a historic site,
and the restaurant caters all events held here. The cooking
emphasizes regional foods based on classic nouvelle preparation.*

LIMITATIONS/RESTRICTIONS

Any event held here must include food and beverage service.

LEAD TIME FOR RESERVATIONS

*May and October are the most popular months. Call for
availability.*

RATES

*Your food and beverage charge covers the use of the site. Rates
for food and beverage are extremely variable, depending upon
the type of function you hold and how many people are
attending. Call for further information.*

FACILITIES FOR THE HANDICAPPED?
YES NO SOME
          X

*The first floor, including the restrooms, is accessible to the
handicapped.*

THE NATIONAL AQUARIUM

U.S. Department of Commerce Building
14th and Constitution Avenue, N.W.

Washington, D.C. 20230
202/377-2826

A lively setting for any assembly

Clownfish and gar fish and sharks, oh my! Green eels, an alligator and deadly piranha! Yes, they're all here, as well as many other water creatures—the built-in entertainment for your party at this most unusual of all meeting sites in Washington.

Your event goes along swimmingly from the start: You enter the aquarium by descending a flight of stairs washed in blue waves of color. Sounds of crashing waves play in the background. The staircase leads into the aquarium's long entrance hallway, which is dotted with free-standing tanks, a Touch Tank and educational graphics. The hallway, in turn, leads to the aquarium proper, a circular room whose walls are lined with more than 60 tanks. The illuminated fish tanks provide most of the lighting for the two rooms and the dim atmosphere reinforces the feeling that you have arrived underwater.

Believe it or not, you can hold not only receptions at the aquarium, but banquets, too. Standing or sitting, you'll have quite a view. There are more than 1,000 fish on display and it is fascinating to see the variety: transparent fish and colorful fish, fish without eyes and fish that fly, fish that kiss and fish that kill. If you're in the mood to learn a fact or two, you can watch the aquarium's educational films about different bodies of water.

For small daytime meetings, or to expand the space available during your evening functions, the Crab Cove room is also available. This room lies off the aquarium's entrance hallway and features large windows overlooking the Commerce Department courtyard and a display of mounted tropical fish along its blue walls.

The National Aquarium is the oldest public aquarium in the country. It was started in Woods Hole, Massachusetts, in 1873 and transferred to its current location in 1932. The aquarium in Baltimore is called the "National Aquarium in Baltimore" and has no affiliation with the facility in Washington.

CAPACITY

Reception: 300
Banquet: 150 (an adjacent cafeteria can be made available to accommodate an additional 500 people provided Aquarium's recommended caterer is used.)
Small meeting or luncheon: 15

LOCATION

In the Federal Triangle, within walking distance of both the White House and the Washington Monument.

FOOD/BEVERAGE

You can use the aquarium's recommended caterer or choose your own, self-contained caterer.

LIMITATIONS/RESTRICTIONS

Music is permitted but animal health considerations may limit volume. You are required to hire the aquarium's security guards for your event.

LEAD TIME FOR RESERVATIONS

One to two months.

RATES

A $500 membership in the National Aquarium Society (a private nonprofit organization) entitles you to an evening's use of the aquarium. Security is an additional cost of $12 per hour.

FACILITIES FOR THE PHYSICALLY HANDICAPPED?
YES NO SOME
X

NATIONAL DEMOCRATIC CLUB

30 Ivy Street, S.E.

Washington, D.C. 20003

202/543-2035

Democrats' hangout on the Hill

The Democratic Club is the dining and meeting choice of Senators and Congressmen, Congressional Staff and party officials from Washington and around the nation.

You can rent one or more of the club's three floors or just one of its six rooms. The club recently underwent an extensive renovation, and its new decor is a fashionable mix of rose, gray, mauve and burgundy furnishings, brass fixtures and dark woodwork.

The club room on the first floor is large and dimly lit and features a bar and grill. Against one wall, a fireplace has been converted into an attractive copper and wood wine closet; mirrors cover the other walls. On the second floor, cherrywood bar stools stand up to a brass-topped mahogany bar in the open reception area. Right next to this spot is a pleasant, rose-colored and paneled conference room. A partition divides the room into two private meeting areas, when needed.

The O'Neill Room on the third floor, a dining room, has burgundy banquettes, dusky rose walls and brass chandeliers. Glass doors at one end of the room lead to a balcony overlooking Capitol Hill. Adjoining the O'Neill Room is a formal conference chamber.

The rooms range in size, from a second floor partitioned compartment that can accommodate 35 to 40, to the third floor O'Neill Room/conference room combination that can accommodate 250.

(Republicans, see the Capitol Hill Club listing.)

CAPACITY

Reception: 25–400
Banquet: 25–150
Meeting: 45 per room

LOCATION

Two blocks east of the U.S. Capitol building.

FOOD/BEVERAGE

The club caters all functions but will work with you to plan your menu.

LIMITATIONS/RESTRICTIONS

You must be a member or be sponsored by a member to hold a function here.

LEAD TIME FOR RESERVATIONS

One to two weeks, but call for availability. The club accepts reservations up to six months in advance.

RATES

$25 charge for fewer than 25 people at a catered function. Costs vary for events without food service.

FACILITIES FOR THE PHYSICALLY HANDICAPPED?
YES NO SOME
     X

NATIONAL 4-H CENTER

7100 Connecticut Avenue
Chevy Chase, Maryland 20815
301/961-2809

A campus facility without distractions

The first thing you'll notice about the National 4-H Center is that, with its sweeping front lawn and stately buildings, it looks like a college campus. In fact, from 1903 to 1950, this was the site of the Chevy Chase Junior College.

The 30 conference rooms range in size and can be set up to meet the needs of your group. Almost every room carries a name—for example, the Missouri Room or the Oklahoma Room—indicating the state whose 4-H Foundation sponsored its unique furnishings. These rooms display works created by artists who hail from that particular state. If you meet in the Oklahoma Room, you'll see Indian art and if you meet in the Ohio Room, you'll see an Ohio painter's six-foot-high, 74-foot-long mural depicting the history and physical aspects of Ohio.

For the most part, the conference rooms are utilitarian meeting areas that provide tables, chairs and any tools you need, such as screens, flip charts, blackboards and podiums. Audiovisual equipment is available at a nominal charge. Many of the conference rooms have especially decorative features. The Missouri Room, for instance, features brass chandeliers and walnut paneling.

If you plan to stay overnight at the Center, you should know that there are different types of bedrooms available. Attractive twin bedrooms feature private bath, television, telephone, daily maid service and linens. Four-person dorm bedrooms feature two bunk beds with central bath, daily maid service and linens.

Although this facility is a get-down-to-business sort of retreat, it also provides an opportunity for recreation. You can go for walks on its $12\frac{1}{2}$ secluded and wooded acres, play pool, volleyball and video games. If you want, the Center can arrange off-site entertainment for your group, such as tours of Washington or dinner theater reservations.

CAPACITY

Reception: 50 to 500
Banquet: 500
Meeting: 25 to 650
Lodging: 630

LOCATION

Just outside and north of Washington, D.C. The district Metro buses stop right in front of the Center on Connecticut Avenue.

FOOD/BEVERAGE

The National 4-H Center offers a full-service cafeteria with individually served or buffet-style luncheons and banquets, receptions, refreshment breaks, box lunches and other special services as requested.

LIMITATIONS/RESTRICTIONS

The National 4-H Center is a nonprofit educational organization whose primary purpose is to serve its members, alumnae and professional staff. The Center rents its facilities year-round to groups whose missions are similar to the Center's, that is, not-for-profit and educational in purpose.

LEAD TIME FOR RESERVATIONS

Call for availability.

RATES

Call for rates. The Center prefers to discuss rates with the individual client.

FACILITIES FOR THE PHYSICALLY HANDICAPPED?
YES NO SOME
X

OATLANDS

Leesburg, Virginia
Mailing address: Route 2, Box 352
Leesburg, Virginia 22075
703/777-3174

A grand old Virginia home

Shortly after you arrive here, you start to wonder what it would be like to own Oatlands. Who can resist? The wonderful Greek Revival mansion bursts with character. Its many rooms are furnished with antiques that are not only beautiful but comfortable. The surrounding grounds keep the outside world at a distance while the formal terraced garden keeps you entranced with its unexpected turns, mysteriously hidden enclosures and endlessly varied flowers, plants and trees. The only thing Oatlands seems to be missing is occupants, and that's where you come in.

For a reasonable fee, you can rent the grounds and the first two floors of the house for your exclusive use. The bedrooms on the second floor are roped off for viewing purposes only, and so is the octagonal drawing room on the first floor, but that still leaves the large entry hall, the dining room, breakfast room, library, "morning room" and upstairs hall at your disposal. A rustic carriage house on the grounds is also available for meetings.

Everything you see is noteworthy. The tall white pillars of the facade, for example, are actually oak-sheathed walnut tree trunks painted to look like plaster. The capitals at the top of the pillars were designed by Oatlands' creator, George Carter, great grandson of famous Virginia plantation owner "King" Carter. Furniture on the first floor is a mix of Louis XIV, XV and XVI; the second floor furniture is all American.

George Carter started building the house in 1804 and altered it as styles changed. Carter designed and planted the original garden as well. When William Corcoran Eustis and his wife, Edith, bought Oatlands in 1903, they renovated the mansion and restored and expanded the garden. All of the furniture in the house (except for the dining room's massive sideboard) belonged to the Eustises. The tea house, the bowling green, the reflecting pool and the rose garden reflect the Eustis family's handiwork in the garden. Oatlands is now a property of the National Trust for Historic Preservation.

CAPACITY

Reception: 75, inside; up to 500 with the use of a tent on the lawn
Banquet: 20, inside; up to 500 with the use of a tent on the lawn
Fairs, exhibitions on the grounds: more than a thousand
Meeting: 15 to 20 (in the mansion), 75 (in the carriage house)

LOCATION

Approximately six miles south of Leesburg, Virginia, on Route 15. From Washington: Take Route 7 West to Leesburg, then go south on Route 15 to Oatlands; or take I-66 to Route 50 West to Gilbert's Corner, then go north on Route 15.

FOOD/BEVERAGE

Oatlands has one preferred caterer and a list of alternate approved caterers. If you would rather use another caterer, you may submit the name of your caterer to Oatlands for review and approval. Oatlands requires that the caterer also handle the rental of tents and tables and chairs. A kitchen is available in the basement and is equipped with a stove, refrigerator, double ovens, sinks, freezer and work tables.

LIMITATIONS/RESTRICTIONS

Oatlands is available evenings only, March through December. Smoking is prohibited inside the mansion and carriage house. Hard liquor may be served for no more than two hours and beer and wine for no more than five hours. A certificate of insurance is required to rent Oatlands. You must rent a tent when the number of your party exceeds the interior capacity.

LEAD TIME FOR RESERVATIONS

At least four months.

LOCATION

From the Beltway: Take Exit Route 66 West to Route 123 (Chain Bridge Road). Follow Route 123 South to Main Street. Go left on Main Street and left again on University Drive. Old Town Hall is at the corner of Main Street and University Drive.

FOOD/BEVERAGE

You may choose your own caterer.

LIMITATIONS/RESTRICTIONS

No smoking is allowed in the building.

LEAD TIME FOR RESERVATIONS

Call for availability.

RATES

Call for rates. (At this writing, new rates were being considered to reflect building enhancements brought about by the renovation.)

FACILITIES FOR THE PHYSICALLY HANDICAPPED?
YES NO SOME
X

THE PHILLIPS COLLECTION

1600 21st Street, N.W.

Washington, D.C. 20009

202/387-2151

A feast for the eyes

At The Phillips Collection, you can feast your eyes on Bonnards and Renoirs at the same time you're enjoying your fete. This is Washington's beloved museum of modern art and the oldest one in the United States.

You can rent the main building, the main building and its annex, or simply a conference room for your event. The museum was once the private home of the Phillips family, so the setting is as eye-catching as the art.

First floor rooms in the Georgian Revival main building feature oriental carpets, pastel walls and exquisite, small pieces of furniture. The Jacobean music room on the same floor serves as the banquet hall and lecture room, and it is breathtaking: Dark-stained, quartered oak paneling covers the walls; heavy wood columns support the hall at one end; and the high ceiling is poly-chromed plaster molding.

The rooms upstairs are more gallery-like, with tan wall-to-wall carpeting, white-painted and fabric-covered walls and little furniture. On the lower level is the conference room/cafe. This room is decorated in a California bar–style, with light wood tables, chairs and floors, lots of light and plants. The Phillips Collection wing is closed for renovation and will reopen in mid-1989.

But enough about the design of the place, it's the paintings that will most thrill you here. You'll view Daumiers and Cezannes, Klees and Braques, Kokoschkas, Gauguins, Sisleys and Morisots—and more.

One other tip: Be sure to look at the fireplaces; each one is unique and a work of art in itself.

FOOD/BEVERAGE

You make your own catering arrangements, although the staff will provide light refreshments, i.e., snacks and soft drinks, for a minimal fee. The ballroom is equipped with a commercial-grade kitchen.

LIMITATIONS/RESTRICTIONS

For evening functions (other than wedding receptions) you must hire one police officer for every 150 people who attend.

LEAD TIME FOR RESERVATIONS

Up to a year, but call for availability.

RATES

Monday through Thursday, 8:00 A.M. to 4:00 P.M.: $10 per hour for nonprofit organizations and $17.50 per hour for all other groups, for a minimum of three hours; after 4:00 P.M.: $425 for any organization for seven hours' use. Friday: $650 for any type organization for seven hours' use; Saturday: $700 for any type organization for seven hours' use; Sunday: $600 for any type organization for seven hours' use. A $200 refundable deposit is required to reserve the ballroom on the weekend. The cost for security is $15 per hour.

FACILITIES FOR THE PHYSICALLY HANDICAPPED?
YES NO SOME
X

ROCKVILLE CIVIC CENTER MANSION

603 Edmonston Drive
Rockville, Maryland 20851
301/424-3184 or 424-8000, ext. 401

New use for an old house

Rockville wasn't always the booming metropolis you see today. At the beginning of this century, Rockville was idyllic countryside dotted with the summer houses of wealthy Washingtonians. In fact, the Civic Center Mansion used to be one of them. Yes, this stone plantation house on 100 acres, this mansion with its first floor conservatory, dining room, lounge and library and second floor servant's quarters and countless bedrooms, was simply a rich cardiologist's summer retreat.

Well, *you* can use it anytime of the year, although not the whole house. The entire first floor is available for social events and the occasional business conference, and two rooms on the second floor are available for meetings.

The central foyer dates from 1838, when a Maryland judge and abolitionist constructed the original building. Most of the mansion was built in the 1920s by the summering Lyon family. The result is a gracious reception area on the first floor that joins the lounge to the foyer to the library. Wide entryways seem to extend the space of one room into the next. Next to the library is the green, marble-floored conservatory—a great space for dancing; behind the lounge is the walnut-paneled dining room. These rooms are all large and made for entertaining in grand fashion.

The two upstairs conference rooms are small, furnished with tables and chairs and have a modern feel to them. Down the hall are the Rockville Municipal Art Gallery rooms, which you are welcome to visit.

Besides the mansion, you can rent two other facilities on the estate: the 500-seat F. Scott Fitzgerald Theatre and the Social Hall. The theater offers more than just a stage area; there's an orchestra pit, sophisticated sound and light systems, a lobby, ticket booth and dressing rooms. The Social

Hall, located on the lower level of the theater, measures 90 feet by 60 feet and may be rented for meetings, receptions and dinners.

CAPACITY

Reception: 225 (mansion), 250 (social hall)
Banquet: 50 (mansion—standup buffets only), 235 (social hall— seated dinner)
Conferences: 60 (mansion), 500 (theater), 250 (social hall)
Performances: 500 (theater)

LOCATION

Near the junction of Route 28 and Rockville Pike in Rockville, Maryland.

FOOD/BEVERAGE

The mansion allows only standup buffets, but you can choose your own caterer. A kitchen is available in both the mansion and the social hall for warming and cooling foods. The mansion's kitchen also has a microwave oven.

LIMITATIONS/RESTRICTIONS

Tents are not permitted outside and cooking is not permitted inside. You're not permitted to bring additional tables and chairs into the mansion.

LEAD TIME FOR RESERVATIONS

Social events: Rockville residents—up to one year in advance; Nonresidents—not more than nine months in advance. (Rockville residents get a three-month lead over nonresidents in reserving the mansion.) Meetings: Call for availability.

RATES

Rates are structured according to use and category of user. For example, a Rockville civic organization would pay $43 for three-hours' use of a conference room in the mansion during the week, while a nonresident would pay $1,095 for five hours' (plus two hours for setup) rental of the entire mansion for a social event. Rental of the theater costs $472 for residents and $599 for nonresidents for four hours' use. Rental of the social hall costs $399 for residents and $668 for nonresidents.

FACILITIES FOR THE PHYSICALLY HANDICAPPED?
YES NO SOME
X

SELMA PLANTATION

Off Route 15
Leesburg, Virginia 20075
Mailing address: Postal Route 4, Box 656
Leesburg, Virginia 22075
703/777-1885

A view seldom seen

Stand on the front porch of Selma and behold beauty as far as your eye can see: miles and miles of green pastures, rolling Virginia hills and farmland stretching to the Blue Ridge Mountains on the horizon. The Selma mansion is itself situated on one of those Virginia hills, two miles off the main byway, so nothing comes between you and the view.

Grandeur of a man-made sort greets the eye when you take a look at the mansion. You'll probably spy the white columned and porticoed edifice of the Classic Revival structure in the distance as you travel the winding road to its entrance. Now, as you enter the mansion's first floor rooms, all available to you along with the grounds, you see the magnificence close up.

Dominating the first floor is the great hall, which measures approximately 45 by 27 feet and is the largest room in the house. The hall boasts its own set of pillars, a 14-foot ceiling and an open staircase that winds to a landing overlooking the hall before spiraling up to the second and third floors. The alcove created by the stairway/balcony is an ideal spot in which to set up a bar or band. (The hall is often used for dancing.)

On one side of the hall is a roomy, dark-wood paneled dining room while on the other side are two large, beige-colored living rooms and a smaller, dark-wood paneled study. Each of these rooms is handsomely furnished with old portraits and paintings, working fireplaces and comfortable furniture. Wide entryways connect the rooms to

160

each other and to the hall, and long front windows provide that stupendous view as the backdrop to your affair.

Selma was built by a wealthy banker in 1900 and its land was farmed until 1970. The current owners of Selma actually live here and open their home to you most of the year for special events.

CAPACITY

Reception: 250 (inside), 350 (inside and out)
Banquet: 175 (inside), 300 (inside and out)
Garden party: 350
Meeting: 175 (in the great hall) to 250 (throughout)

LOCATION

Four miles north of Leesburg and 40 miles northwest of Washington. From the Beltway, take the Route 7 West exit and follow Route 7 almost to Leesburg. Take the Route 15N exit toward Frederick. Selma's drive is the first left past the sign for Whites Ferry.

FOOD/BEVERAGE

Selma provides a list of recommended caterers; you're welcome to choose from that list or one of your own. A kitchen is available for warming and cooling, but not for cooking.

LIMITATIONS/RESTRICTIONS

No specific restrictions; review your requests with the management.

LEAD TIME FOR RESERVATIONS

At least one month in advance.

RATES

Weekdays: starting at $500. Weekends: starting at $1,500. Rates vary widely depending upon the type of event you're holding and how many people are attending, so call for further information.

FACILITIES FOR THE PHYSICALLY HANDICAPPED?
YES NO SOME
X

SEWALL-BELMONT HOUSE

144 Constitution Avenue, N.E.
Washington, D.C. 20002
202/546-1210

Museum for the women's movement

Hold a function at the Sewall-Belmont House and you're on the site that fostered today's women's movement. Not only that, but the mansion is one of the oldest on Capitol Hill, dating from the late 1600s. The red brick structure is an amalgam of architectural styles, from colonial farmhouse to French Hansard, reflecting the changes made to the house over the course of 300 years.

Two of its floors and a large, enclosed garden are yours for events. Want to dance? The garden's brick terrace makes a great outdoor dance floor. Want to dine? A tent on the lawn in summer and the sunporch in winter provide perfect banquet areas. Want to confer or simply kick back and gab? The whole house is good for that.

All the rooms in the house are handsomely furnished. Like its architecture, however, the house's furnishings represent cross-period styles and the preferences of the various occupants. The best thing to do is to have a docent take you around to give you the history of both the house and the women's movement.

You'll find out, for example, that the green upholstered rosewood sofa and chairs in the drawing room were made by slaves during French colonial times; that the floors were stained their near-black color in Victorian times; that Alice Paul, the author of the Equal Rights Amendment, led the early fight for its passage from this house; and that the house has served as headquarters for the National Women's Party since 1929.

CAPACITY

Reception: 100 to 125 (house alone), 500 (house and garden)
Banquet: 50 (house alone), 350 (house and garden)
Meeting: 50

LOCATION

On Capitol Hill, across the street from the Supreme Court Building.

FOOD/BEVERAGE

You must select a caterer from the Sewall-Belmont's approved list. The kitchen may be used to warm or cool foods, but not for initial preparation of foods.

LIMITATIONS/RESTRICTIONS

Tents are required for all outdoor functions. Smoking is allowed in the sunporch and outside. Red wine is prohibited. Parking is available for events everyday from 4:00 P.M. to 10:00 P.M.

LEAD TIME FOR RESERVATIONS

One to two months, but call for availability.

RATES

$1,500 (considered a donation); $1,350 of the $1,500 is tax-deductible. $1,500 covers all service charges, but not rental charges for tents or tent lighting.

FACILITIES FOR THE PHYSICALLY HANDICAPPED?
YES NO SOME
X

THE SPIRIT OF WASHINGTON
AT PIER 4

6th and Water Streets, S.W.

Washington, D.C. 20024

202/554-8000

Make waves at your next event

Watch as your group unwinds aboard a boat that cruises the Potomac. *The Spirit of Washington* encapsulates the experience of an ocean-going luxury liner into a few pleasurable, memorable hours on the river.

From the stream-lined vessel's open-air deck or the two windowed lower decks, you have a clear view of Washington's monuments and Old Town Alexandria's colonial homes. Meanwhile, the boat's galley is sending up a feast, the bar is serving up drinks and the two live bands are serenading you with songs from the last four decades. During dinner cruises, local talent—who have been masquerading as your waiters and waitresses—perform a Salute to Broadway Revue. And, oh yes, there's dancing.

Designed inside to resemble a deep-sea cruise ship, the *Spirit of Washington* is decorated with plants, aquamarine carpeting, linen-covered tables and beige-cushioned seats. You can rent just a deck or the whole boat for a brunch, lunch, dinner, dance cruise or even a meeting.

The *Spirit of Mount Vernon*, a smaller version of the *Spirit of Washington*, cruises the Potomac daily on excursions to George Washington's historic home and may be rented for special charters.

CAPACITY

Reception: 500 (Spirit of Washington); *250 to 300* (Spirit of Mount Vernon)
Banquet: 415 (Spirit of Washington); *the* Spirit of Mount Vernon *is not available for sit-down affairs.*

LOCATION

Off Maine Avenue, at Pier 4 on the waterfront in southwest Washington.

FOOD/BEVERAGE

The Spirit of Washington *and the* Spirit of Mount Vernon *cater their own events. If you rent the entire* Spirit of Washington, *you can request a menu suited to your group's tastes. Otherwise, the* Spirit of Washington *has a set menu that in 1987 included a choice of chicken, flounder or steamship round; rice, potatoes, green beans, salad, rolls and dessert. The* Spirit of Mount Vernon *always serves a set menu of fingerfood, which in 1987 included cheese, fruit and vegetable platters.*

LIMITATIONS/RESTRICTIONS

The Spirit of Mount Vernon *is only partially enclosed and therefore available from the end of March to the end of October.*

LEAD TIME FOR RESERVATIONS

Three to six months, but call for availability.

RATES

Spirit of Washington: *a minimum of 160 people is required to reserve the small deck, 190 people to reserve the large deck, and 350 people to reserve the entire boat. The rates per person are as follows: lunches- $14.95; Sunday brunches—$16.95; moonlight cruises—$10; dinners—$23.95 (Sunday through Thursday) and $28.95 (Friday and Saturday). These rates include meal and entertainment but not bar charges. Inquire about rates for breakfast and special events charters.* Spirit of Mount Vernon: *$2,100 for a three-hour cruise, plus $5 a person for meals. If you choose to have an open bar, the charge is $12.60 per person.*

FACILITIES FOR THE PHYSICALLY HANDICAPPED?
YES NO SOME
   X

STATE DEPARTMENT ANNEX

(formerly the Iranian Embassy)
3005 Massachusetts Avenue, N.W.
Washington, D.C. 20008
202/232-1023

Middle Eastern opulence on Embassy Row

Don't be fooled by the name of this site. Sure, State Department employees work here now, but they didn't always. This large, marble-fronted building that occupies a prime address on Embassy Row was itself once the embassy of the Iranian government.

Now you can host your own embassy party in the ballroom and courtyard on the first level. From the entrance, you walk back to a reception area and through French doors, into the inner courtyard. A large, blue-tiled fountain dominates the middleground and a garden surrounds the courtyard. If you look up, you see the mosque next door. Although a tree grows in each corner of the courtyard, this is not a shaded area, so for a summer party you might want to rent a tent.

Through another set of French doors, the courtyard connects to the ballroom. This is a long, high-ceilinged room where Iranian decorative flourishes still remain. An elaborate blue and mirror-tiled design borders the room and crowns the ceiling. There's a Persian carpet on the floor and a profusion of plants.

CAPACITY

Reception: 400
Banquet: 250
Garden party: 200 to 250

LOCATION

On Embassy Row, in northwest Washington, near the Massachusetts Avenue access to Rock Creek Parkway.

FOOD/BEVERAGE

The staff here does all the catering for your event. You can request any food you like.

LIMITATIONS/RESTRICTIONS

The rooms are available on Friday evenings after 5:00 P.M. and all day Saturday and Sunday.

LEAD TIME FOR RESERVATIONS

At least one month, but call for availability.

RATES

$250 for fewer than 50 people; $500 for more than 50 people, for a period lasting as long as you like.

FACILITIES FOR THE PHYSICALLY HANDICAPPED?
YES NO SOME
   X

STRATHMORE HALL ARTS CENTER

10701 Rockville Pike
Rockville, Maryland 20852
301/933-7422

Fine art, refined setting in Rockville

Some houses, like some people, have presence, and Strathmore Hall is one of them. Cars whiz past on the road below and shoppers converge on the sprawling mall down the street, but poised on a hill above it all, Strathmore Hall maintains its pleasant peace.

Notice first the exterior: a turn-of-the-century, red-brick mansion surrounded by 11 green acres that include an English sculpture garden. Columned porticoes crown the mansion's entrance and a patio.

Step inside and be equally impressed. You are standing in a marble-floored foyer lit with brass torchieres. The ceiling is glass, set in intricate latticework. Go right, into the marvelous music room where a light-wood floor contrasts with dark-wood paneled walls.

Go left from the foyer and you're in the dining area, painted pale pink and cream. A chandelier sparkles above the room and a long, built-in plant stand overflowing with greenery extends across a wide front window.

Behind these front rooms are a cozy library; a cheery, peach-tinted main hall leading to the patio; and three galleries exhibiting the works of area artists. All eight of these first floor rooms, as well as a kitchen, are at your service when you rent Strathmore.

CAPACITY

Reception: 250 (inside), 400 (with a tent)
Banquet: 70 in one room, 120 throughout the first floor
Meeting: 60

LOCATION

From the Beltway: Take the Rockville Pike (Route 355) exit, going north, and travel on Rockville Pike about .5 mile. Strathmore Hall is located next to the Grosvenor Metro station, .5 mile south of White Flint Mall.

FOOD/BEVERAGE

You choose your own caterer. A large kitchen on site is equipped with a warming oven, freezer, refrigerator, double sinks and lots of counter space.

LIMITATIONS/RESTRICTIONS

Smoking is prohibited in the galleries.

LEAD TIME FOR RESERVATIONS

One year for Saturday and Sunday events; four months for events on other days.

RATES

From $1,000 to $1,500 for a seven-hour period.

FACILITIES FOR THE PHYSICALLY HANDICAPPED?
YES NO SOME
X

STRONGHOLD MANSION

7901 Comus Road

Dickerson, Maryland 20842

301/869-7846

A dream house in the mountains

When you call for directions to Stronghold Mansion, the building superintendent first asks whether you know how to get to "the mountain." This should tell you, if you haven't already guessed, that Stronghold is at a small remove from Washington, D.C. If you're of the opinion that getting there is half the fun and, on top of that, if the day of your event should turn out to be fine and sunny, then you couldn't ask for anything more than this ride through the country that ends up at Stronghold Mansion.

You'll notice as you pull up to Stronghold that it's built into a hill. That hill is really the base of said mountain, Sugarloaf by name. Although rental of the mansion entitles you to roam all of its three floors and the grounds, your function will center in the two large and beautiful rooms at the back of the house, both of which open onto the exquisitely landscaped mountainside lawn.

There's the dining room on the first floor, magnificent with paneled walls and a teak wood floor. The room has all the right touches: antique candelabras, gold-framed mirrors and corner hutches displaying delicate old china. Only standup buffets are allowed in the mansion, but you may carry your food outside and sit on chairs set up on the lawn. This peaceful setting presents you with a view of a gazebo, reflecting pool and lots and lots of trees.

On the second floor is the stunning ballroom, which measures 22 by 60 feet. The ceiling is 16 feet high. At one end of the room lie a piano and organ and space for dancing; at the other end is a comfortable arrangment of sofas and chairs. Full-length French casement windows topped by fanlights line the walls.

If you take a walk thought the rest of the house, you'll

find that most of the other rooms are bedrooms and all are furnished with antiques. Stronghold was the dream house of a Chicago tycoon named Gordon Strong. He bought Sugarloaf Mountain and started building the mansion in 1912. By the time Strong died in 1957, only a third of his planned mansion had been completed—the part that stands today.

CAPACITY

Reception: 150
Garden party: 300

LOCATION

About 40 miles from the center of Washington, D.C. From the Beltway: Take Exit 35, I-270, to the Hyattstown exit. Circle under I-270 and go west on Route 109 to Comus. Take a right on Route 95 and follow the road to the mansion. For a more scenic route, follow River Road in northwest Washington all the way to Route 190, then follow Route 190 past Seneca to Route 109; follow Route 109 to left on Route 28 and then right on Route 95.

FOOD/BEVERAGE

You arrange your own catering and bar service. The mansion's kitchen is equipped with a stove and refrigerator, but you must supply your own utensils and dishes.

LIMITATIONS/RESTRICTIONS

The first floor and the grounds are the only places where you may take food. You must rent a tent if your party exceeds 150 people and you must supply your own tables and chairs. The mansion is available only on weekends.

LEAD TIME FOR RESERVATIONS

At least three to four months, but call for availability.

RATES

$700 for the use of the whole house for as long as you like, but there's no spending the night. Rates may increase in 1988.

FACILITIES FOR THE PHYSICALLY HANDICAPPED?
YES NO SOME
   X

THE THOMAS LAW HOUSE

461 N Street, S.W.
Washington, D.C. 20024
202/944-4508

Historic home on the Washington waterfront

Given the importance of the Potomac River to Washington's history, you'd think there would be many 18th century houses still standing along the waterfront, but there aren't. The Thomas Law House is one exception.

It sits back on a wide green lawn, a lone but handsome example of Federal-period architecture. You walk across the original cobblestone courtyard and enter through the elegant fanlight-topped door. The five unfurnished rooms on three floors that you find inside are available for a variety of purposes.

Two first-floor rooms, one of which was once a bedroom, the other the main parlor, are suitable for meetings and stand-up receptions. Second-floor rooms are used for banquets and dancing. Step out to the terrace adjoining the "green room" and you have a wonderful view of the Potomac, the Washington Monument and other historic sights. A modern room on the third floor is available for meetings.

Each of the rooms bears some distinguishing interior feature that you seldom see anymore: intricate crown molding, black marble Greek Revival fireplaces and rounded inset windows. The rooms have been painted in colors that are thought to accurately represent the tastes of the period.

The spacious front and side lawns are available for functions as well.

CAPACITY

Reception: 150
Banquet: 75
Garden party: 300, with tents
Meeting: 40 to 50 in one room

173

LOCATION

Directly across the street from the Spirit of Washington *at Pier 4, off the cul-de-sac at the end of Water Street, S.W. From Maine Avenue, turn right on 7th Street, then left on Water Street. Follow Water Street to the cul-de-sac.*

FOOD/BEVERAGE

The Thomas Law House contracts exclusively with one caterer but will consult with you to plan your menu. There are full kitchens on both the second and third floors, and a dry kitchen on the first floor.

LIMITATIONS/RESTRICTIONS

Dancing and dance music are allowed only on the second floor. Events must conclude by midnight.

LEAD TIME FOR RESERVATIONS

At least six months.

RATES

Rates range from $400 for a four-hour meeting to $1,000 for an eight-hour social event.

FACILITIES FOR THE PHYSICALLY HANDICAPPED?
YES NO SOME
   X

TOUCHDOWN CLUB

2000 L Street, N.W.

Washington, D.C. 20036

202/223-1542

A sporting place to rally your troops

All right, sports fans, here's a place for you. The Touchdown Club is teeming with team spirit—for the Washington Redskins, for the University of Maryland's Terrapins, for any groups, jocks, and nonjocks alike, that choose to gather here. If you are a true sports fan, you want to keep your eyes open, because famous athletes drop in all the time.

An outside flight of stairs in busy, downtown Washington leads you down into the below-street-level club. Once inside, you find the atmosphere to be, well, clubby. It's dark; there's an underlying hum of quiet conversations; photos of past club presidents line the walls of the hallway, and portraits of famous football players hang in every room.

In all, there are six areas available for events. There's a barroom furnished with black club chairs, banquettes and booths, and, of course, a bar and bar stools. Just off the bar is the Redskins Room where you can hold small luncheons or meetings and study the pictures of famous Redskins. Another small room is the Collegiate Room which is most suitable for more formal, private functions. This room features plaid-cushioned chairs, college memento plates donated by members, and a huge framed black-and-white photograph of the first college football game in history—in 1869, between Rutgers and Princeton.

The Maryland, Virginia and Washington Rooms open onto each other to accommodate large groups and are suited to many purposes. Redskins players often hold press conferences here, and the space is also good for meetings, banquets and receptions.

CAPACITY

Reception: 400
Banquet: 280
Meetings: 15 to 250

LOCATION

Four blocks from the Farragut North Metro station in downtown Washington.

FOOD/BEVERAGE

The club handles all food and beverage arrangements, but will work with your group in planning the meal.

LIMITATIONS/RESTRICTIONS

No specific restrictions; discuss your requests with management.

LEAD TIME FOR RESERVATIONS

At least a week or two. Fall is the club's busiest season.

RATES

The club does not charge for room rentals, only meals. Luncheon: $15 per person; dinner: $25 per person.

FACILITIES FOR THE PHYSICALLY HANDICAPPED
YES NO SOME
X

An elevator at street-level takes you down to the club.

WASHINGTON DOLLS' HOUSE & TOY MUSEUM

5236 44th Street, N.W.
Washington, D.C. 20015
202/244-0024

Charming collection enlivens the past and parties

If you're looking for a site that offers an icebreaking atmosphere and a social history lesson on the side, this is the place. Try as you might to stick to business, you'll find it hard to resist peering at the miniature furnishings and clever playthings on display here. These are antiques, and the collection gives you a fascinating glimpse at past trends in architecture, decorating, fashion and pastimes.

A cluster of seven rooms on the first floor, a second floor Edwardian tea room and a lot behind the museum comprise the available rental space. Because most of the lighting for the downstairs area emanates from the display cases lining the walls, these rooms have an intimate feel about them. Potted palms and antique ice cream tables cheerily decorate the upstairs tea room.

And everywhere you glance are small treasures: an elaborate 1890 Mexican doll-mansion complete with chapel (and priest) and terra cotta pottery; a mid-nineteenth century house from Burford, England, featuring early English wallpapers; a 1903 New Jersey seaside hotel; and an 1850s peddler doll hawking wares of candles, veil pins and buttons. Should you have questions about the collection, a staff person attired as an Edwardian maid is on hand at every function.

CAPACITY

Reception: 100 inside, 300 with tent
Banquet: 24 inside, 150 with tent

LOCATION

The museum is located in upper northwest Washington, one block west of Wisconsin Avenue.

FOOD/BEVERAGE

You're free to choose your own caterer. The museum has a small kitchen equipped with a refrigerator, freezer and hot plate.

LIMITATIONS/RESTRICTIONS

Smoking is prohibited in the museum. The museum is available for events from 5:00 P.M. to midnight and all day on Mondays.

LEAD TIME FOR RESERVATIONS

At least several weeks, but call for availability.

RATES

$50 per hour, with a four-hour minimum. This rate entitles you to use the whole first floor for your event.

FACILITIES FOR THE PHYSICALLY HANDICAPPED?
YES NO SOME
     X

THE WOMAN'S NATIONAL DEMOCRATIC CLUB

1526 New Hampshire Avenue, N.W.
Washington, D.C. 20036
202/232-7363

A jewel of a clubhouse

You'd be hard pressed to find a more gracious meeting place than this clubhouse. Once the home of a well-to-do opera singer, the mansion now has other purposes, one of which is to be "a place of tolerance, where minds may meet." Certainly the club's finely appointed interior and genial atmosphere create the appropriate setting.

With its peaked-roof turret and many-sided shape, the club's exterior resembles a small castle. Inside, there are ten rooms on two floors, as well as a garden, that are available for functions. Each room is furnished with portraits, paintings, antiques and political memorabilia donated by members, distinguished Democrats and friends.

Perhaps the most notable of these rooms, for meeting purposes, are the Marjorie Merriweather Post parlor, the Adlai Stevenson Room and the Sam Rayburn Lounge. The parlor is furnished with antique furniture, a piano and an oriental rug and makes an inviting reception area. For larger luncheons, meetings and dinners, you'll want to use the Stevenson Room, which is a pleasant space with yellow walls, a raised stage, and all sorts of meeting accoutrements. The Rayburn Lounge serves mostly as a cocktail and luncheon room, is decorated in rose tints and has a bar at one end. Its walls are hung with pictures, cartoons and documents dramatizing historic moments in Speaker Rayburn's career.

The other rooms and the garden are choice spots for small meetings or for catching moments of repose. Don't miss the library, an engaging room filled with books by and about prominent Democrats; the Daisy Harriman Room, named for one of the club's famous founders and furnished with art objects and drawing room pieces from her estate; and the lovely brick-paved and enclosed garden.

CAPACITY

Reception: 300
Banquet: 225
Meeting: 200

LOCATION

In the Dupont Circle area of northwest Washington, across the circle from the Dupont Circle Metro station.

FOOD/BEVERAGE

The club has its own in-house catering service and prepares all food but will work with you to plan your meals.

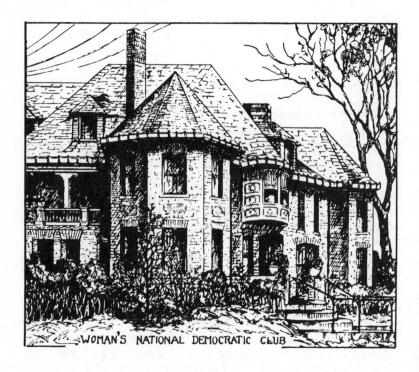
WOMAN'S NATIONAL DEMOCRATIC CLUB

LIMITATIONS/RESTRICTIONS

Rental of the clubhouse for events is restricted to members or to groups who have been sponsored by members.

LEAD TIME FOR RESERVATIONS

The staff recommends that you call for availability.

RATES

Rates vary depending upon the type of event, the space used and the day and time of function.

FACILITIES FOR THE PHYSICALLY HANDICAPPED?
YES NO SOME
X

The first floor is accessible to the handicapped.

WOODROW WILSON HOUSE

2340 S Street, N.W.
Washington, D.C. 20008
202/387-4062

Home to Wilson after the White House

Picture this: Woodrow Wilson skipping down the aisle of a train on his honeymoon night whistling the early 1900s tune "Oh You Beautiful Doll." It isn't a very presidential image, but it certainly is an endearing one. It is the personal side of our 28th president that you learn about when you rent the house he retired to at the end of his second term.

This red-brick, Georgian Revival townhouse offers you the use of five rooms, a terrace and the garden, all preserved much as they were when the Wilsons lived here in the 1920s. You can hold intimate banquets in the same room where Wilson dined (but only when he was properly attired in a dinner jacket). After dinner, you may want to stroll out to the red-tile terrace for a little night air or retire to the library for some quiet business talk. The library is a dark, cozy room filled with books and mementos of Wilson's hobbies and presidency.

Or maybe you'd like to hold court in the drawing room, where Wilson stood at the window to acknowledge the crowd that had gathered to honor him on Armistice Day in 1923. Many of the drawing room's furnishings were wedding gifts given to the Wilsons, including a French Gobelin tapestry from the French ambassador and a marble-mosaic portrait from the Vatican. You are welcome to use the Wilson's Steinway grand piano.

The charming solarium completes the suite of rooms available for events on the main floor. A large interior window overlooks the house's central stairway while the solarium's other windows provide a view of the garden.

The two-level, stone wall–enclosed garden area is a spacious place to gather for receptions and banquets during the warmer months. A modern conference room is available on the house's first floor for small meetings, lunches and dinners.

CAPACITY

Reception: 75 (house), 300 (house and garden)
Banquet: 36 (house), 100 (house and garden)
Garden party: 200
Meeting: 45

LOCATION

One block off Embassy Row (Massachusetts Avenue) in northwest Washington.

FOOD/BEVERAGE

You must choose a caterer from the museum's approved list. A kitchen is available for warming and cooling foods.

LIMITATIONS/RESTRICTIONS

Smoking, red wine, dancing and amplified music are prohibited in the house. You can rent the conference room for daytime functions, but the other rentable areas are available only in the evening. Evening functions must end by 11:00 P.M. The house is not air-conditioned.

LEAD TIME FOR RESERVATIONS

One to six months, depending on the season. Fall and spring are the busiest seasons.

RATES

Main floor and terrace: $1,500; main floor and garden: $2,500; main floor dining room: $2,000; conference room: $500. You are also requested to contribute a $100 membership fee. These rates cover a maximum of four hours' use.

FACILITIES FOR THE PHYSICALLY HANDICAPPED?
YES NO SOME
               X

Sites for
500 to 1000 People

ARMORY PLACE

925 Wayne Avenue

Silver Spring, Maryland 20910

301/585-5564

Silver Spring's central attraction

Smack dab in the middle of Silver Spring is where you find Armory Place, a red brick fortress-like building with a grand plaza for a front yard. As its location indicates, Armory Place is a community center—but one that's available to the Washington community at large.

There are eight rentable areas inside the three-story structure. Seven of these rooms resemble classrooms, with their fluorescent lights, functional tables and chairs, and, for the most part, tile floors. The rooms are ideally suited for meetings and seminars, although other uses are also possible. The smallest space accommodates 25 for a meeting; the largest accommodates 200.

The best room in the house is on the second floor. Room 204 is really a huge hall measuring 96 by 58 feet. Its many large windows command great views of downtown Silver Spring. The egg-crate style ceiling is high and the floor is covered in reddish orange wall-to-wall carpeting. This is a grand space that you can use for any purpose—from dances to banquets to business meetings. If you hold a dance here, the Armory will rent a portable dance floor to you that suits the size of your group. The dance floor is available in three-foot-square sections, the largest floor measuring 30 square feet and accommodating approximately 300 people.

CAPACITY

Reception: 700

Banquet: from 24 in one of the smaller rooms to 320 in the large hall

Meeting: from 25 in one of the smaller rooms to 600 in the large hall

LOCATION

In the heart of Silver Spring, 1½ blocks from the Silver Spring Metro station.

FOOD/BEVERAGE

You must choose a caterer from Armory Place's approved list. There is a small kitchen equipped with a refrigerator, stove and counter space. Alcoholic beverages are permitted subject to permission by the Department of Parks, the laws of the state of Maryland and license requirements of Montgomery County.

LIMITATIONS/RESTRICTIONS

Ticket sales at the door are not allowed. "Bring your own bottle" functions are not permitted. Armory Place is available between 8:30 A.M. and 11:00 P.M. Sunday through Thursday and between 8:30 A.M. and 1:00 A.M. Friday and Saturday.

LEAD TIME FOR RESERVATIONS

One year in advance for the large hall; three to six months for the meeting rooms.

RATES

Rates range from $35 for rental of the smallest room for six hours' use any time, to $600 for rental of the large hall on a Saturday for six hours' use, plus $50 for each additional hour.

FACILITIES FOR THE PHYSICALLY HANDICAPPED?
YES NO SOME
X

Everywhere except on the third floor.

THE CAPITAL CHILDREN'S MUSEUM

800 Third Street, N.E.
Washington, D.C. 20002
202/675-4126

A wonderland for children of all ages

Pack your curiosity and your sense of wonder and you're all set to have fun at the Capital Children's Museum. Here you'll discover exhibits that are just as fascinating for adults as they are for children.

You can rent the whole museum or parts of it for use after public hours, and portions of it for use in daytime.

The Communication Hall is a great place to get your colleagues to loosen up. The two-level hall demonstrates the methods by which human beings have expressed themselves, from the Ice Age to today's Computer Age. Here you can view reproductions of the ancient drawings made by cavemen, make a movie for a zoetrope (an early version of a movie projector), listen to a form of language known as pig latin, learn how hobos communicated, explore a radio recording studio, use an 18th-century working press and learn how much information can be stored on a disk, a computer chip and in the human brain.

The Mexico exhibit, which occupies most of the area known as International Hall, allows you to visit a miniature Mexico, complete with a city street and a Sierra mountain cabin. Here you can learn to make tortillas, listen as the voice of an archaeologist explains the significance of a pre-Columbian burial mound, learn how Mexicans live, and pick up a little Spanish.

The Birthday Party Room and the auditorium are available during the day, and so is the Banquet Room when no exhibit is on display there. These three rooms are plain, functional areas that barely hint at what lies beyond in the main museum. The Banquet Room is situated next to the kitchen, has a red and white tile floor and long windows; the auditorium features a stage, fold-up chairs and yellow walls.

187

If you rent one of these spaces for a daytime event, you can tour the museum as individuals after paying the admission charge. At night, however, you're entitled to tour only the space you've rented, so your best bet is to rent one or all of the exhibit areas.

CAPACITY

Reception: 1,000 (whole museum)
Banquet: 100 (maximum in one room)
Meeting: 150 (auditorium)

LOCATION

Three blocks from Union Station and Capitol Hill.

FOOD/BEVERAGE

You're free to choose your own caterer. A small kitchen is available for warming and cooling.

LIMITATIONS/RESTRICTIONS

Smoking is prohibited in the museum. There is limited parking available, although arrangements can be made to rent a parking lot directly across the street.

LEAD TIME FOR RESERVATIONS

At least 90 days, but call for availability.

RATES

Rates range from $1,000 to $5,000, depending upon which space or spaces you rent.

FACILITIES FOR THE PHYSICALLY HANDICAPPED?
YES NO SOME
X

CAPITAL CLUB

The Capital Centre
Harry S. Truman Drive
Landover, Maryland 20785
301/350-3111

Entertain, then be entertained

You're in good company, if you choose to hold an event here. The Capital Club has hosted an inaugural reception for Ronald Reagan, a fundraiser with Frank Sinatra and parties for the likes of Stevie Wonder and Diana Ross.

The Capital Club is located within Washington's premier sports/entertainment facility, the Capital Centre. If you're reserving the club for a function, you must also reserve tickets for the show, which means you can catch up with each other and catch a performance, and it's all in a day's work. The Capital Centre is mammoth and books acts that draw mammoth crowds, such as Kenny Rogers and Fleetwood Mac.

The club consists of one large room and adjoining bar and is suitable for any type of event, from a meeting to a dinner/dance. The club's interior has been renovated to further enhance this sophisticated setting. A portable dance floor, piano, public address system, podium and television monitors are among the meeting essentials that are always available.

CAPACITY

Reception: 700
Banquet: 350

LOCATION

Going south on the Beltway, take Exit 17A to right on Landover Road and right again on Harry S. Truman Drive. Going north on the Beltway, from Virginia or the District, take Exit 15A to right on Central Avenue, to left on Harry S. Truman Drive.

FOOD/BEVERAGE

The Capital Club has its own in-house catering service and will work with you to plan your meal.

LIMITATIONS/RESTRICTIONS

The club's availability is subject to the Capital Centre's schedule. For instance, the club is open only to season ticketholders whenever the Washington Bullets (basketball), Capitals (ice hockey), or Georgetown University's basketball team have a game at the Capital Centre. The club does not open for wrestling, hard rock concerts or truck shows.

LEAD TIME FOR RESERVATIONS

Two to three months, but call for availability.

RATES

There is no room rental fee. Food and beverage rates start at $5 a person and go up from there, depending upon the desires of the group. Tickets to the Capital Centre's entertainment range in price from $4.75 to $75 a person.

FACILITIES FOR THE PHYSICALLY HANDICAPPED?
YES NO SOME
X

THE CORCORAN GALLERY OF ART

17th Street and New York Avenue, N.W.
Washington, D.C. 20006
202/638-3211

Magnificence captured in a museum

The only drawback to holding an event at the Corcoran
Gallery of Art is that eventually you have to leave. The
museum is a dream palace of art, architecture and atmosphere. Frank Lloyd Wright is said to have called it the best-
designed building in Washington. After your event, you'll
probably call it one of your favorite Washington sites.

Receptions and banquets take place in the double atrium,
on the atrium bridge and in the area called the Clark Landing. The double atrium is the focal point of the museum—
it's a two-story, temple-like hall, up a flight of stairs from
the entrance. Fluted columns punctuate this great space,
rising 40 feet from the marble floor to skylight ceiling. The
bridge, overhead, horizontally spans the middle of the
atrium, gracefully distinguishing the second level from the
first.

The wide, wide marble staircase that takes you to the
upper atrium leads you first to a landing and the back part
of the museum. Proceed through the spectacular rotunda
and you arrive at Clark Landing. This is a small, walnut-
paneled room with enormous charm. A staircase winds up
one side, a gallery overhangs from above—the perfect niche
for a string quartet or harpist—and exquisite 17th-century
Loire Valley tapestries hang on the wall, along with paintings depicting the story of Joan of Arc. Clark Landing is
available for receptions.

The Corcoran, which is most famous for its extensive
collection of American masterpieces, may open some or all
of its galleries for browsing, depending upon the type of
event you're holding. The galleries are located all around
the upstairs atrium and extend way beyond the south side
of the building, on both floors. Some of the works to revel

191

in include Frederic Remington's sculpture, *Coming through the Rye*, Rembrandt Peale's huge portrait of George Washington, and modern art by Andy Warhol, Mark Rothko and others.

An auditorium is also available for lectures, chamber music and other small performances. This blue-tinted semicircular room has a round stage and a concert grand Steinway piano.

CAPACITY

Reception: 1,000
Banquet: 400
Auditorium: 193

LOCATION

Within walking distance of the White House, one block west. The museum faces onto the Ellipse.

FOOD/BEVERAGE

You choose your own caterer and the Corcoran approves your choice.

LIMITATIONS/RESTRICTIONS

Red wine, dancing and fundraising are prohibited. Events in the gallery may take place at any time on Monday and from 6:30 P.M. to midnight any other day, except Thursday. Events may be held in the auditorium at any time, subject to the Corcoran's schedule. (The Corcoran School of Art frequently uses the auditorium, especially during the day.) Smoking is not permitted in the galleries. The director of special events reviews each request for use of the Corcoran and makes a recommendation to the trustee committee for approval of an event.

LEAD TIME FOR RESERVATIONS

At least four to five months.

RATES

Only corporations and organizations that have contributed a $7,500 membership fee are eligible to reserve the Corcoran for a function. In addition, there are service fees: $250 plus $150 per 100 guests, and an overtime charge of $150 for each hour beyond five hours. You must also purchase a certificate of insurance for the use of the museum.

FACILITIES FOR THE PHYSICALLY HANDICAPPED?
YES NO SOME
        X

The double atrium is accessible to the handicapped.

FRYING PAN SCHOOLHOUSE

2709 West Ox Road
Herndon, Virginia 22071
703/437-9101

Historic landmark in a park

Funny name, Frying Pan. One story has it that early pioneers searching for gold in a creek came upon some Indians frying up meat in a pan stolen from them. The settlers killed the Indians, retrieved their pan and appended the name "frying pan" to the creek and the surrounding land.

The schoolhouse is old, but not that old—it dates from 1911. The red-brick structure has a two-story-high ceiling, white walls, large windows and pine floors. There are three meeting/reception rooms, each measuring 19 by 26 feet, and a demonstration kitchen. These light-filled, unfurnished rooms are ideal for off-site business meetings and receptions.

The schoolhouse lies in Frying Pan Park, which includes two other facilities for events: an Activity Center and an outdoor equestrian center. The Activity Center's main feature is its sand floor riding arena, which seats 800 people and is equipped with a public address system. The center is best suited for such activities as soccer games, chili cookoffs and concerts, whereas the equestrian center is available strictly for horseriding. The park grounds, which are mostly open, unshaded pastures, are available as well.

CAPACITY

Reception: 100
Park picnic: 150
Meeting: 100
Activity Center event: 800

LOCATION

From the Beltway: Take Exit 9 or 9A, Route 66 West, to Route 50 West to right on Centreville Road in Chantilly to right on West Ox Road to park entrance on left.

194

FOOD/BEVERAGE

You make your own food and beverage arrangements.

LIMITATIONS/RESTRICTIONS

Smoking is prohibited in the building. Alcohol consumption is prohibited outside the building. The schoolhouse is not air-conditioned. The building is available all year round, everyday from 8:00 A.M. to midnight. An alcoholic beverage use permit is required to serve alcohol.

LEAD TIME FOR RESERVATIONS

Several months for the schoolhouse, and as much as a year in advance for the Activity Center. The site is popular year-round.

RATES

Rates for renting the schoolhouse and the grounds each range from $60 for a four-hour function held by a county nonprofit organization to $115 for a four-hour event held by a noncounty profit organization. The fee structure for rental of the Activity Center varies widely, depending upon its use and the length of time it is rented, so you should call for those rates.

FACILITIES FOR THE PHYSICALLY HANDICAPPED?
YES NO SOME
      X

The schoolhouse does not have facilities for the physically handicapped but other park areas do.

NATIONAL MUSEUM OF WOMEN IN THE ARTS

1250 New York Avenue, N.W.

Washington, D.C. 20005

202/783-5000

A museum made for entertaining

Even before it opened in April 1987, the museum stirred up controversy: Will a separate showcase bring long-deserved recognition to women artists or will art segregated from works by men be taken less seriously? Whichever opinion you hold, one thing's indisputable: The museum itself seems made for entertaining.

Housed within a huge Renaissance-Revival style structure are four spaces for renting: the Martin Marietta Great Hall located on the first floor and mezzanine, third-floor galleries, a fourth-floor board room and a fifth-floor auditorium.

The lofty Martin Marietta Great Hall is a masterpiece of tricolored marble brought over from Turkey and laid down by Turkish workers. There are over 11,000 square feet of space here and it's all marble, and so is the sweeping double staircase that leads to the mezzanine level. Three immense, cut-crystal chandeliers brilliantly illuminate the hall for banquets and receptions.

For smaller affairs, the third-floor gallery area is available. This multi-purpose space works best for receptions, given the way the exhibit rooms break up the space. Here resides the museum's permanent collection of more than 300 works by women—paintings, sculpture, graphic arts and photography, from the 16th century to the present. Also on this floor is the State Gallery, which features a changing exhibit of art created by women from a particular state.

The auditorium has mauve, gray and rose furnishings and features a two-story-high ceiling, marvelous acoustics, state-of-the-art audiovisual equipment and a platform stage framed within a wide arch.

The board room is simply furnished for business use and

holds approximately 20 people for a luncheon. Other areas, such as the special exhibit galleries on the second floor, may be available for events, on occasion and by special arrangement.

CAPACITY

Reception: 1,000 (great hall and mezzanine); 400 (third floor gallery)
Banquet: 500 (great hall and mezzanine); 125 (third floor gallery)
Meeting: from 20 in the board room to 200 in the theater
Performance: 200 (auditorium)

LOCATION

Two blocks from the White House in downtown Washington, at the corner of 13th Street and New York Avenue. One block from the Metro Center Metro station and within walking distance of the D.C. Convention Center.

FOOD/BEVERAGE

The museum has a list of recommended caterers but allows you to choose your own. The museum is equipped with a full caterer's kitchen, with easy access to the loading dock and freight elevators.

LIMITATIONS/RESTRICTIONS

Smoking is permitted in the great hall, but may not be allowed in other parts of the museum, depending upon the exhibits being shown. The great hall and mezzanine area is available any day for evening events and on Mondays for luncheons. The auditorium is available for day and evening functions. Gallery areas are available for evening functions.

LEAD TIME FOR RESERVATIONS

Event scheduling is subject to the museum's own schedule. Call for availability.

RATES

Great hall and mezzanine: $7,500; third floor gallery: $3,500; auditorium: on a sliding scale, from $800 to $1,250, depending on the audiovisual equipment used; board room: call for contribution amount.

FACILITIES FOR THE PHYSICALLY HANDICAPPED?
YES NO SOME
X

OXON HILL MANOR

6901 Oxon Hill Road
Oxon Hill, Maryland 20745
301/839-7782

Meet in grand manner at the manor

Staging an event at Oxon Hill Manor, some ten miles or so from the White House, whets your appetite for the good life. Everywhere you look, inside and out, you see beauty, and that beauty is yours, if only for a few hours.

Before you take possession of the five first-floor rooms available to you within this neo-Georgian house, proceed directly to the covered and wide brick terrace that runs along the back of the house. From there you find the manor's enormous green lawn sloping down into a woods that catches the Potomac on the horizon. To the side of the house lie lovely gardens. You're free to stroll the grounds or you can rent the grounds for a tented event, but only in conjunction with the rental of the house.

Back inside, you see that the drawing room, library and dining room each capture a portion of the breathtaking view through their tall French doors that open onto the terrace. Each of these rooms is spacious, high-ceilinged and has its own distinct character. The rose-colored drawing room is elegant with its huge stone fireplace, finely carved woodwork and parquet floor. This is the room usually used for musical entertainment and dancing. Dark wood paneling and tall built-in bookcases lend the library a warm, snug feeling, making it an inviting place to mingle during cocktail receptions. A choice spot for intimate banquets is the dining room, whose peaches-and-cream-colored walls display large Chinese watercolor murals painted on rice paper.

You may also use the spacious, marble-floored foyer for your event; you may have a bar here and use the room to expand your reception area. Down a long hall, past a grand, sweeping stairway is the tea room, suitable for small meetings.

You'll never get to see all of them, but Oxon Hill Manor actually houses 49 rooms. The manor was built in 1928 for American diplomat Sumner Welles. Welles held many esteemed positions during his career, including a term as Under Secretary of State to President Franklin Delano Roosevelt. Roosevelt was one of the many illustrious visitors to Welles's estate.

CAPACITY

Reception: 300 (inside), 800 (inside and in the tented garden)
Banquet: 300 (throughout the first floor rooms), 800 (inside and in the tented garden)
Garden party: 800
Meeting: 40 to 75 in one room

LOCATION

From the Beltway: Take Exit 3A and turn right onto Oxon Hill Road.

FOOD/BEVERAGE

You can choose any caterer who is licensed and insured. The Manor provides a suggested list.

LIMITATIONS/RESTRICTIONS

The garden can be rented only with the use of the house. You must erect a tent on the grounds when the 300-person capacity of the house is exceeded. Use of the house and walk-throughs are by appointment only. The manor is available all year, except for the month of February and part of March.

LEAD TIME FOR RESERVATIONS

At least six months, but call for availability.

RATES

Social functions: $700, Monday through Thursday; $850, on the weekend; and $120 for each additional hour past the usual seven. These rates include the use of the library, dining room, drawing room, foyer and tea room. Rental of just one or two of those rooms for social functions is possible during the week only at a rate of $360 for either the drawing room or the dining room, plus $60 per additional hour over seven, and $480 for the drawing room and library or the dining room and library, plus $80 for each additional hour over seven. The tea room may be rented at a flat charge of $25, with the rental of these other rooms.

Meetings: $30 for the tea room to $120 for the drawing room, for a four-hour period. Overtime charges range from $7 per hour for the tea room to $20 per hour for the drawing room.

There are also service charges for setup, take-down and trash removal, unless you make your own arrangements.

FACILITIES FOR THE PHYSICALLY HANDICAPPED?
YES NO SOME

X

U.S. DEPARTMENT OF AGRICULTURE PATIO

U.S. Department of Agriculture Administration
Building
14th Street and Independence Avenue, S.W., at the
Mall
Washington, D.C. 20002
202/447-8482

An Italian courtyard on the Mall

You'll forget you're in a government building when you throw an affair at the Department of Agriculture's patio. In fact, you may even forget what country you're in or what century it is. The patio has the look and feel of a 16th-century Italian courtyard.

One large skylight encloses the patio area from way up high, filling the room with light and creating a feeling of wide open space. The room is approximately 90 feet by 56 feet, and its interior walls are two stories high. The walls themselves are extraordinary: they're made of yellow marble and tan brick, and tall arched entryways have been carved into them on three sides. A balcony runs around the top of these walls on the second floor. In the middle of the variegated green and purple slate floor stands a beautiful, blue tile fountain spouting water. Great green plants bloom all around the room, providing a simple but charming embellishment, and flags of the 50 states salute the area from the sidelines.

This is an amazingly lovely space in which to entertain, and all the more so given the rental fee—it's free. That is, there is no charge to rent the room, but there are service charges: for the electrician and for cleanup, heating/air conditioning, restroom supplies and lighting. A piano is available and the patio is equipped with a sound system.

203

CAPACITY

Reception: 600
Banquet: 350
There is no minimum number of people required to reserve the patio, but the staff recommends at least 100 since the space is so large.

LOCATION

On the Mall, at 14th and Independence Avenue, S.W.

FOOD/BEVERAGE

You arrange for the caterer and beverage service. It's up to you, too, to arrange for tables and chairs and anything else you need.

LIMITATIONS/RESTRICTIONS

Use of the patio is limited to federal government and private, nonprofit organizations on a first-come, first-served basis, but priority is given to government organizations.

LEAD TIME FOR RESERVATIONS

At least one month.

RATES

Service charges: Electrician (if requested)—$20 per hour 8:00 A.M. to 4:30 P.M., weekdays, and $30 per hour after 4:30 P.M. on weekends or holidays; heating—$77.50 per hour; air conditioning—$63 per hour; restrooms—$15; floor cleaning—$240.50; lighting—$25 per hour.

FACILITIES FOR THE PHYSICALLY HANDICAPPED?
YES NO SOME
X

Sites for more than 1000 People

GUNSTON HALL

Lorton, Virginia 22079
703/550-9220

Meet at the home of a founding father

One of the things you learn when you tour George Mason's spectacular estate is that the statesman was instrumental in shaping our Constitution and is known as the Father of the Bill of Rights, yet he rarely joined in the fray. Mason preferred, instead, to work at home, and who can blame him? Gunston Hall is a garden of paradise along the Potomac River.

Mason's Georgian-style mansion sits on 550 acres that include extensive formal gardens, nature trails, outbuildings, an herb garden, meadows and the contemporary Ann Mason Visitors Center. Available for rent are a modern meeting facility in the Ann Mason Building and a designated outdoor area, usually the tree-lined meadow, on the grounds.

The meeting room boasts a cathedral ceiling and has brick walls on which hang original 18th-century oil portraits of Mason's descendants. You can hold a meeting here using the facility's podium, microphone, screen and projector, then clear away all evidence of business and start partying. Glass doors lead to a brick-paved, inner courtyard where, in warm months, you can set up a bar around the center fountain or in one of the tree-shaded corners.

Whether or not you rent the grounds, you really must take a stroll outdoors. The wonderful gardens contain only plants found in colonial days; the 12-foot-high English boxwoods that form a center allée were planted by Mason himself. You can hike the mile to the Potomac River via a nature trail.

Rental of the Ann Mason room or the grounds includes a special guided tour of Mason's mansion. Built in 1755, the mansion is a masterpiece of architectural symmetry. Its interior is furnished as historians believe it would have been in Mason's day, and some of its original features still remain. Note especially the beautiful, hand-carved woodwork in the formal parlor and, in the study, the writing table on which Mason composed the Virginia Declaration of Rights, which became the model for the U.S. Bill of Rights.

CAPACITY

Reception: 350 (in the Ann Mason Building)
Banquet: 150 (in the Ann Mason room)
Garden party: 2,000
Meeting: 150 (in the Ann Mason room)

LOCATION

Travel south on I-95 to Exit 55, Lorton. Follow the signs to Gunston Hall.

FOOD/BEVERAGE

You must choose a caterer from Gunston Hall's approved list. The site has a full kitchen and provides rental equipment, if needed.

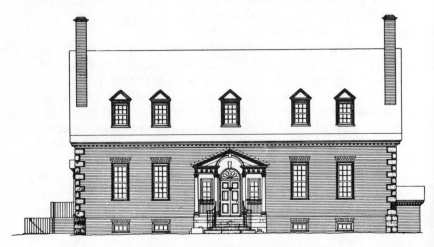

LIMITATIONS/RESTRICTIONS

Events cannot take place in the mansion and food and beverage are prohibited there. If your party exceeds the capacity of the Ann Mason room, you must rent the grounds. Although a tent is not required with the use of the grounds, the staff strongly advises you to rent one, to allow for inclement weather.

LEAD TIME FOR RESERVATIONS

Weekend events: call a year in advance.
Weekday events: call one to two months in advance.

RATES

Ann Mason room: Lunch-$150; day meeting-$250; evening affair-$500; wedding reception-$700.
Grounds: $1,500. Rates cover any period of time up to 11:00 P.M., after which the charge is $100 per hour for the use of the grounds and/or the Ann Mason room. Rental of the grounds includes the use of the Ann Mason room when it has not been rented by another group. There is a $1 per person charge for admission to the mansion, whether or not a tour is conducted.

FACILITIES FOR THE PHYSICALLY HANDICAPPED?
YES NO SOME
X

The Ann Mason Building and the grounds are accessible, but the mansion is not.

J.R.'S FESTIVAL LAKES

Route 773
Leesburg, Virginia 22075
Mailing address: 8130 Watson Street
McLean, Virginia 22102
703/821-0545

A barn for business, picnic areas for pleasure

Tired of meeting in windowless conference rooms? Bored at the thought of another office party held in the company cafeteria or at the same old bar down the street? If you want to add some pizazz to your function, take your group to J.R.'s, where as many as 5,000 conferees can be accommodated.

J.R.'s lies at the end of a country road in a private wooded setting with lakes. You can kick off your meeting, sales presentation or seminar in the renovated Club Barn. The barn is open on three sides and provides you with tables and benches, a stage, a public address system and lighting that can be dimmed for audiovisual presentations. Horse shoes, a straw-strewn floor and bales of hay scattered about reinforce the rustic atmosphere.

At the close of the meeting, you can get down to the more serious business of having fun. J.R.'s offers just about any kind of outdoor activity you can imagine: volleyball, badminton, horseshoes, swimming, fishing, golfing, hiking and boating. The site is so large that tractor-drawn wagons transport you from one activity area to another.

J.R.'s helps you plan your event by providing you with artwork for invitations, promotional material, lists of activities, maps, menus and names of recreational vendors. They help arrange entertainment acts for you, as well.

CAPACITY

Reception: 5,000
Banquet: 1,500 (barn space, plus adjoining area that can be tented)
Meeting: 1,500 (barn space, plus adjoining area that can be tented)
Picnic: 5,000

LOCATION

From the Beltway: Take Exit 10 West to Route 7 West. Go 21 miles on Route 7 to Route 15 North toward Frederick. After traveling .3 miles, exit right to Route 773. Go 1.4 miles and turn left at J.R.'s.

FOOD/BEVERAGE

J.R.'s rustles up barbecue-style feasts for most functions, although other menus are available upon request.

LIMITATIONS/RESTRICTIONS

Use is seasonal, from April through October. Music must meet the facility's sound control level. A minimum of 50 persons per group is required to reserve the site during the week; a minimum of 100 persons is required on the weekends.

LEAD TIME FOR RESERVATIONS

Call for availability. Weekdays and evenings are usually easier to reserve.

RATES

Rates range from $12 to $20 per person, depending upon the menu selection. Food and beverage costs cover the use of the entire site. Media equipment is available at an extra cost.

FACILITIES FOR THE PHYSICALLY HANDICAPPED?
YES NO SOME
X

The barn is accessible to the handicapped.

MORVEN PARK

Old Waterford Road
Leesburg, Virginia 22075
Mailing address: Route 3, Box 50
Leesburg, Virginia 22075
703/777-2414

Virginia hunt country's historic estate

The Morven Park mansion is so well hidden within its 1,200 acres of woods and pastures that when it suddenly looms before you, a huge, white stucco structure dominated by a Greek Revival portico, you gasp in astonishment. Wait 'til you see the inside.

First, however, you should take a look at the grounds. There are seven acres of formal gardens here, including boxwoods, a variety of flowers and a hedge-shielded reflecting pool with spouting fountains. Picture the privacy: You stand sipping cocktails in a secluded spot within a secluded park. The whole world is kept at bay.

You can rent the grounds alone, the house and grounds together, or just the house for functions. There are six rooms on the mansion's first floor that are available to you, and be prepared—they're unbelievable. Flemish, 1640s tapestries cover the 17-feet-high walls of the entry hall, known as the Renaissance Great Hall. This is the only room in which sit-down banquets may be held. Behind the Great Hall lies the paneled Trophy Room where the stuffed heads of elk, deer, moose and mule look on as you conduct meetings. Other rooms include the Jacobean-styled dining room, the French drawing room, the light-filled library and the Museum of Hounds and Hunting, the only collection of its kind in the world.

The Morven Park mansion started as a fieldstone farmhouse in 1781 and grew in grandeur when owned first by a governor of Maryland, Thomas Swann, in the 19th century, and then by a governor of Virginia, Westmoreland Davis, in the early part of this century.

CAPACITY

Reception: 150, inside; up to 2,500, outside
Banquet: 50, inside; 400, outside
Garden party: up to 2,500
Meeting: 50

LOCATION

Morven Park is located at the western end of Leesburg. From Washington: Go west on Route 7, straight through Leesburg. Follow the signs and turn right on Morven Park Road and left on Old Waterford Road.

FOOD/BEVERAGE

Morven Park has a list of approved caterers from which you must choose. A warming and cooling kitchen is available on the premises.

LIMITATIONS/RESTRICTIONS

Smoking is prohibited inside the mansion. Groups renting the mansion must obtain a certificate of insurance. Morven Park mansion is available all year round, anytime from Labor Day to

211

Memorial Day, and after 5:00 P.M., Memorial Day to Labor Day.

LEAD TIME FOR RESERVATIONS

At least one month.

RATES

Rates start at $2,500 for the use of the grounds and the house, for either a day or evening event.

FACILITIES FOR THE HANDICAPPED?
YES NO SOME
    X

The first floor is accessible to the handicapped.

NATIONAL BUILDING MUSEUM

Pension Building
Judiciary Square, N.W.
Washington, D.C. 20001
202/272-2448

Grand place to have a ball, inaugural or otherwise

You don't have to be an architect to appreciate the masterful design of the National Building Museum. Look at its exterior—the building stretches beyond the length of a football field and its red brick edifice gleams as if the bricks were laid just yesterday. Now regard the interior. An Italian Renaissance courtyard takes up almost the entire first floor of the building and a peaked roof encloses the court 159 feet above your head.

The Great Hall, as the courtyard is called, is the museum's main rental space. Its vast dimensions make for a dramatic setting for large receptions, dinners and other gala events. The hall's staggeringly beautiful features heighten the drama. Eight marbleized Corinthian columns face each other on either side of the court's central fountain. The pale pinkish-orange columns are eight feet across and 75 feet high and are the largest Corinthian columns in the world. All four floors overlook this magnificent space—via arcaded loggias on the first and second floors, a parapet on the third floor and a wrought iron balcony on the top floor. The roof capping the courtyard is painted blue to suggest the sky.

A suite of three adjoining rooms on the second floor provides a smaller but elegant area for receptions and banquets. Floor-to-ceiling doors in one room open onto the arcade overlooking the Great Hall. An auditorium on the first floor offers you a conference/seminar space equipped with a stage and audiovisual apparatus.

213

Washingtonians know the National Building Museum as the old Pension Building because it was built in 1882–1887 to house Pension Bureau offices. From the interconnecting rooms off the central court, clerks dispensed funds to wounded veterans and their survivors of the American Revolution, War of 1812, Civil War, Spanish-American War and World War I. If it seems an unlikely office building, it's because the architect, Montgomery Meigs, had an enlightened view of construction. In modeling the building after

an Italian palace plan, Meigs had two purposes in mind: to create an open, airy, light-filled and healthy working environment and to provide the capital with a grand space for entertaining. Starting with Grover Cleveland's Inaugural Ball held here in 1885 even before the building was completed, the site has hosted some of the biggest and best parties in town.

The structure opened as the National Building Museum in 1985. The museum is free and open to the public from 10:00 A.M. to 4:00 P.M. Monday through Friday and Noon to 4:00 P.M. weekends and holidays.

CAPACITY

Reception: 140 (suite), 1,600 (Great Hall)
Banquet: 140 (suite), 1,600 (Great Hall)
Meeting: 135 (auditorium)
The Great Hall is so large the staff recommends that you have at least 200 people in your party when you rent it.

LOCATION

In downtown Washington, on F Street between 4th and 5th Streets, N.W., directly across from the Judiciary Square Metro station, F Street exit.

FOOD/BEVERAGE

You must choose a caterer from the museum's approved list.

LIMITATIONS/RESTRICTIONS

Smoking is prohibited in the galleries. Red wine is prohibited. To reserve the museum for an event requires the approval of the National Building Museum committee. Organizations are limited to one museum event per year.

LEAD TIME FOR RESERVATIONS

At least six months, but call for availability.

RATES

Nonprofit organizations: $3,600; corporations: $8,500. These rates allow you to use the museum from 8:00 A.M. to 1:00 A.M. the following day. The central court of the Great Hall, however, is off limits until after 4:00 P.M. Additional service charges for *items such as security and cleanup vary according to size of your event and number of hours from set-up through strike-time. The second floor suite rents for $500 and the auditorium rents for $450; service charges for the use of these two spots amounts to about $200. The suite and auditorium are available both during the day and evening.*

FACILITIES FOR THE PHYSICALLY HANDICAPPED?
YES NO SOME
X

NATIONAL PRESS CLUB

529 14th Street, N.W., 13th Floor

Washington, D.C. 20045

202/662-7500

High up in the heart of Washington

It's arguable that there's no better place to put your finger on the pulse of Washington, or the pulse of the country for that matter, than here at the National Press Club. On any given day, you'll see the people you just read about in the morning newspaper, or people you're going to read about in tomorrow's. All kinds of famous figures, from President Reagan to Jane Fonda to Jerry Falwell, use the Press Club as a forum, and the world's best journalists are here to cover them.

Aside from the celebrity scenery, the Club's quarters are sensational, as well. Wrapped around an atrium on the 13th floor of the National Press Building are handsomely furnished rooms accented with marble, mahogany and brass. Available for events are four meeting rooms (also used for press conferences), two lounges, a dining room, and a ballroom. Each of the rooms is adaptable to serve many purposes.

The meeting rooms are located along a hall that overlooks the atrium. Each is named for a distinguished American journalist and is equipped with communications and audiovisual systems. Three of the rooms can be joined or used individually.

On the other side of the atrium lie the areas best suited for social events. You can hold a reception in the First Amendment Lounge or out on the terrace, where you'll view the White House and the Washington Monument. Remember the photograph of Lauren Bacall reclining across the top of a piano being played by Harry Truman? That very piano is here in the Truman Lounge.

The Main Lounge is more formal but comfortable, furnished with overstuffed sofas and a grand working fireplace and flanked on either side by dark-wood bars. This room works well, as is, for a reception or, with the furniture removed, for a banquet and dancing.

Finally, there's the ballroom, a huge hall with two large balconies and an undulating, two-stories-high, paneled ceiling. The ballroom can be partitioned into three separate sections.

CAPACITY

Reception: 15 to 1,500
Banquet: 5 to 480
Terrace party: 15 to 150
Conference: 5 to 500

LOCATION

Two blocks east of the White House and one block west of the Metro Center Metro station, at the corner of F and 14th Streets, N.W.

FOOD/BEVERAGE

The club caters all meals and will work with you to plan your menu.

LIMITATIONS/RESTRICTIONS

To rent the National Press Club, you must be either a member or sponsored by a member.

LEAD TIME FOR RESERVATIONS

About six months, but call for availability.

RATES

Room rates range from no charge for a lunch of 16 people or more, to $1,750 for full-day use of the ballroom. Rates vary depending upon membership status and which room is being rented. Food and beverage costs are extra.

FACILITIES FOR THE PHYSICALLY HANDICAPPED?
YES NO SOME
X

THE PAVILION AT THE OLD POST OFFICE

1100 Pennsylvania Avenue, N.W.

Washington, D.C. 20004

202/289-4224

For dancing, dining and socializing

On New Year's Eve at The Pavilion, you'd find yourselves in a crowd of thousands ringing in the new year. On any other night, however, The Pavilion may be just the spot for your crowd to ring in a new product or a merger, or a new president (The Pavilion has been the site of an inauguration dinner or two).

As you might have guessed, The Pavilion has plenty of space. The old post office is an imposing neo-Romanesque structure, nine stories high. Inside, an enormous inner atrium shoots up to the roof. It is surrounded by offices at the upper levels, and a festival marketplace with specialty retail stores, restaurants and an international food court at the lower levels. When you rent The Pavilion, the stores and restaurants are usually closed and your event takes place in the common area on the bottom two floors.

The lower levels are open areas; from any one of these floors you can see to the next, and wide marble central stairs connect the levels. Looking above the third floor, you see the vaulted glass roof and the original steel girders put in place when the building was constructed in 1899 as the first federal post office. Through the glass roof you might also notice the Clock Tower rising 350 feet on the outside. The Tower offers one of the highest views of the city, second only to the Washington Monument's. The Tower is open in spring, summer and fall from 10:00 A.M. to 11:00 P.M. and in winter from 10:00 A.M. to 5:45 P.M.

With the rental of The Pavilion, you also get to use its stage, dance floor, piano and powerful sound and lighting systems.

CAPACITY

Reception: 2,500
Banquet: 550

LOCATION

Halfway between the White House and the U.S. Capitol on Pennsylvania Avenue, only two blocks from the Mall and five blocks from the Convention Center.

FOOD/BEVERAGE

You can arrange for catering through The Pavilion restaurants or any professional catering company. There is no kitchen but there are two preparation rooms available.

LIMITATIONS/RESTRICTIONS

The Pavilion is usually available for events in the evenings.

LEAD TIME FOR RESERVATIONS

A couple of months, but call for availability.

RATES

$5,000. This rate covers the use of the lower two levels and cleanup charges.

FACILITIES FOR THE PHYSICALLY HANDICAPPED?
YES NO SOME
X

ROSECROFT RACEWAY

6336 Rosecroft Drive
Fort Washington, Maryland 20744
301/567-4000

Put your event on the right track

And they're off! Take your group to the races and watch your event come out a winner.

Actually, you don't have to be betting types to have fun at Rosecroft—the raceway's clubhouse is open in and off-season. (The season runs from mid-October through mid-May.) You find Rosecroft nestled in the hills at the end of a winding tree-lined road. The clubhouse is a three-level, enclosed structure that offers reception space for thousands. In spite of its size, Rosecroft has a warm, clubby feel to it. You can linger in the lobby and learn from the exhibits about such things as the life of the track's founder, William E. Miller, and the birth of the hot dog; or you can proceed to your party in the colorful banner-hung first floor hall or in the mezzanine hall on the second floor, or in the light-filled third floor dining area.

The club's prime attraction is its Terrace Dining Room, on the second and third floors. With room for a thousand, seated, it's one of the largest banquet spaces in the capital area. The huge, glass-fronted room has tiered seating and overlooks the home stretch, so, in season, everyone has a great view of the harnessed trotters and pacers as they strain for the finish line. Doors on all floors of the club lead to outdoor seating by the rail. In addition, almost every table has its own ten-inch color television, just to make sure you don't miss the action. In-season and off-season, Rosecroft is a pretty, secluded spot in which to hold a function.

CAPACITY

Reception: 5,000 (when all three floors are rented)
Banquet: 1,000 seated in the Terrace Dining Room; 3,000 seated on all three floors

LOCATION

From the Beltway: Take Exit 4A and follow the signs.

FOOD/BEVERAGE

The clubhouse caters all functions. It offers a varied menu featuring mostly American and Maryland favorites such as prime rib and crabcakes, but the staff will work with you to plan your menu.

LIMITATIONS/RESTRICTIONS

To use the clubhouse off-season, event insurance is required. Races take place during the evenings only.

LEAD TIME FOR RESERVATIONS

Off-season: three weeks; in-season: two weeks.

RATES

First floor: $2,500; second or third floor: $1,500; entire club: $3,500. These are nonseason rates and do not include food and beverage charges. The average meal costs $17.50 per person. During the racing season, your group pays the dinner charge, but no rental fee. Group packages are available.

FACILITIES FOR THE PHYSICALLY HANDICAPPED?
YES NO SOME
X

SMOKEY GLEN FARM

16407 Riffleford Road
Gaithersburg, Maryland 20878
301/948-1518

Get down to the serious business of barbecue

The barbecue you taste at Smokey Glen Farm has been 30 years in the making. It all started in the 1950s when a man named Sweet had a swell idea: Why not sell barbecued chicken at University of Maryland football games? The idea took off and by 1958 Sweet was not just seriously into barbecuing, but into the barbecue outing business.

Smokey Glen Farm is a social site as well as a business. Located on 73 acres of rolling and wooded hills that back up to Seneca Creek State Park, Smokey Glen provides you with the perfect setting for an outing. There are three picnic areas on the property: the Meadow, the Grove and the Pavilion, each featuring open-air pavilions for seating, and athletic facilities for horseshoe, volleyball, basketball, softball and other games. In addition, the site helps you arrange for a host of other activities, from pie-eating contests to hayrides to square dances.

The staff coordinates your whole barbecue shebang including, most important, preparation of the feast. Charcoal-roasted chicken, prime rib, spare ribs, pig, corn on the cob, lobster bake and charcoal-baked breads and desserts are just some of the farm's sumptuous specialties.

CAPACITY

Daytime picnics and evening parties: from 120 (minimum) to 5,000.
Lobster bakes, business meetings and special menu events: from 50 (minimum) to 250.

LOCATION

From the Beltway: Take I-270 N exit toward Frederick. Follow 270 to the Rockville/Route 28 exit; go west on Route 28 (turn right onto Route 28) and follow until you turn right again onto Riffleford Road and right again into Smokey Glen Farm.

FOOD/BEVERAGE

Smokey Glen handles all food and beverage arrangements.

LIMITATIONS/RESTRICTIONS

Gambling is prohibited. The serving of alcohol is limited to beer and wine for no more than six hours at daytime events. Bar service for evening parties may include hard liquor in addition to beer and wine, but must end by 11:45 P.M.

LEAD TIME FOR RESERVATIONS

Call for availability. Weekday events are usually easier to schedule. The site starts taking reservations in January for the remainder of the year. Repeat customers get first priority.

RATES

Rates range from $11.95 per adult for a daytime picnic to $33.90 per adult for a daytime lobster bake. Rates cover barbecue and beverage charges and the use of the site. Many additional food items are available at an extra charge. There is a $200 service charge for groups numbering fewer than 200 for daytime picnics and for groups under 120 for business meetings.

FACILITIES FOR THE PHYSICALLY HANDICAPPED?
YES NO SOME
  X

TORPEDO FACTORY ART CENTER

105 North Union Street

Alexandria, Virginia 22314

703/838-4199

An artful site on the waterfront

What do you do with a torpedo factory when there's no longer a need for torpedoes? Turn it into a center where artists can work, exhibit and sell their art—what else?

Built in 1918 to manufacture torpedo shell cases, this large three-story building retains its identity as a former factory. Its floors are concrete; original steel railings, exposed pipes and ductwork still stand; lighting fixtures are industrial-style and the walls and columns are painted a plain white.

The intriguing thing about the Torpedo Factory is that its austere design acts as a perfect foil to the rich assortment of arts and crafts displayed in the 85 studios housed here. Through the windows of these artists' spaces you'll see their work in many forms, including painting, ceramics, sculpture, weaving and glasswork.

You can rent the first floor or the entire building for after-hour events. Whatever space you rent, you're free to stroll out to the enchanting deck area behind the center, where you'll discover yourself face-to-face with the Potomac River. The weathered wood benches, a gazebo, old-fashioned ball lights and the marvelous view make the deck itself a terrific place to hold an event. This space does not belong to the Torpedo Factory, however, so if you plan to set up tables here or use the gazebo, you need to call the Alexandria Recreation Department (703/838-4820).

CAPACITY

Reception: 50 to 1,500
Banquet: 30 to 300
Deck party: 200

LOCATION

Seven miles from the U.S. Capitol, fronting the Potomac River in Old Town Alexandria.

FOOD/BEVERAGE

You're free to choose your own caterer. A small, fully equipped kitchen is available. You must obtain liability insurance. The Torpedo Factory staff will advise you about how and where to obtain the needed insurance.

LIMITATIONS/RESTRICTIONS

Alcohol is prohibited on the deck. Your event must end no later than 12:00 A.M. and cleanup must be completed an hour after the event. The center requires that you use its security officer.

LEAD TIME FOR RESERVATIONS

Allow three months to reserve the Torpedo Factory for an event taking place around Christmas or during April or May; allow several weeks to reserve the site at other times during the year.

RATES

The Torpedo Factory charges the following flat rates: main floor—$1,000; entire building—$2,000. The Alexandria Department of Recreation charges $50 per hour for the use of the deck.

FACILITIES FOR THE PHYSICALLY HANDICAPPED?
YES NO SOME
X

WOODLAWN MANOR HOUSE

16501 Norwood Road

Sandy Spring, Maryland 20860

301/585-5564

A 19th-century gem set in Maryland countryside

At first sight of the Woodlawn manor house and surrounding grounds, you notice that the estate has a welcoming appearance rather than an imposing one. The house is large, but not huge. Its architecture is simple Georgian brick with some Victorian touches, not bedecked with columns and porticoes. And though wide-open green pastures encircle the house, a private garden embraces the manor close up, beckoning you to enter the manor's inner circle. Woodlawn is a gracious host of a house awaiting your arrival.

The restored house offers you five rooms on two floors for functions. First-floor rooms include a dining room decorated in 19th-century style; a cozy family room with a large brick hearth and working fireplace, original exposed beams and comfortable furniture; and a long double parlor painted Jamestown blue and white, with brass chandeliers and windows overlooking the lawn. Upstairs are two sitting rooms decorated in the Williamsburg mode.

Outside, you'll find trees shading the house on all sides. Use of the house includes use of the garden, which is enclosed by a hedge of boxwoods, bordered on the inside by rows of multi-colored flowers. A white gazebo provides the perfect covered spot for the band or the bar. The surrounding grounds are available as well. Of interest, too, are several old outbuildings: a log cabin, a late-1800s tenant house and a stone meathouse and dairy.

Woodlawn was built around 1800 by the Thomases, a Quaker family that ran a small boarding school here. The Maryland-National Capital Park and Planning Commission now owns Woodlawn.

228

CAPACITY

Reception: 125, inside; 1,000 or more outside
Banquet: 75
Lawn party: 1,000 or more
Meeting: from 7 to 40 people in one room

LOCATION

From the Beltway: North of Washington, take the Connecticut Avenue exit towards Kensington. Follow Connecticut Avenue to right on Randolph Road. Follow Randolph Road to left on Georgia Road, then a quick right onto Layhill Road. Follow Layhill Road to left on Norwood Road, followed by a right onto the Woodlawn property.

FOOD/BEVERAGE

You must choose a caterer from Woodlawn's approved list. The house has a kitchen equipped with a warming oven, triple sink, refrigerator and freezer.

LIMITATIONS/RESTRICTIONS

Smoking is prohibited inside the mansion, and tents are prohibited in the garden/gazebo area.

LEAD TIME FOR RESERVATIIONS

Three weeks for weekday and evening events and for weekend events taking place from November through March; nine months for weekend events scheduled for April through October.

RATES

Meetings: $35, Monday through Friday, from 8:00 A.M. to 5:00 P.M. The rate covers the use of the house and grounds for seven hours or an entire working day.
Social functions: Fridays, Sundays and holidays—$500; Saturdays—$625; Mondays through Thursdays—$375. These rates cover the use of the house and grounds for a seven-hour period; the overtime charge is $75 per hour.

FACILITIES FOR THE PHYSICALLY HANDICAPPED?
YES NO SOME
X

WOODLAWN PLANTATION

9000 Richmond Highway
P.O. Box 37
Mount Vernon, Virginia 22121
703/780-4000

A picturesque site near the Potomac

If you'd visited here in the early 1800s, you would have seen acres and acres of plantation fields being worked by slaves. A servant would have ushered you into the long, living-room-like hallway where Nelly Custis Lewis, George Washington's foster daughter and the mistress of the mansion, would have greeted you. After dinner, the Lewis family would have entertained you in the music room by playing the pianoforte, harps, guitars and other instruments.

When you visit Woodlawn today, you see acres and acres of beautifully landscaped grounds that include century-old boxwoods, oak and Osage orange trees, a collection of 19th-century roses, two parterres and nature trails. Now, *you* can entertain up to 2,000 of your closest colleagues by holding a tented garden party here.

Or you can hold smaller receptions, banquets or meetings in the mansion's two "hyphens," known as the Reception and Underwood Rooms. The Underwood Room, named for the Alabama senator who lived here in the 1920s, offers formal furnishings: an oriental rug, brass chandelier and working fireplace. The Reception Room is a more casual space with Williamsburg blue and off-white walls, and a nonworking fireplace. Both rooms give on to the front courtyard.

Still another space available for small luncheons and meetings is the downstairs Pub, a rustic room with painted brick walls and exposed beams.

A guide will take you around the mansion during your event and explain the history of Woodlawn, including the fact that the plantation was George Washington's gift to Nelly Custis and Lawrence Lewis, Washington's nephew, upon their wedding. You'll see Nelly's own needlework, vases that were gifts from Lafayette, the house's original, Virginia pine floors and a lot more. Be sure to inquire about the mourning picture on the second floor.

CAPACITY

Reception: 125
Banquet: 100
Garden party: 2,000
Meeting/Luncheon: 40 to 50

LOCATION

Fourteen miles south of Washington, D.C., on U.S. 1 near Mount Vernon.

FOOD/BEVERAGE

You must choose a caterer from Woodlawn's approved list and purchase all your alcoholic beverages from Woodlawn, as well. A caterer's kitchen is available.

LIMITATIONS/RESTRICTIONS

Smoking is permitted only in the banquet rooms and outside. Dancing and amplified music are prohibited in the mansion. You must tent the grounds when the number of your party exceeds the mansion's capacity.

LEAD TIME FOR RESERVATIONS

Call for availability.

RATES

Daytime rates: $400 for rental of either the Underwood or the Reception Room, for a minimum of four hours' use, and $100 per hour after the four-hour mark; $150 for rental of the Pub for up to four hours' use.

Evening rates: $1,200 for up to 200 people, plus $2 a person over 200, for an event held from 5:00 P.M. to 10:00 P.M., and $200 an hour from 10:00 P.M. to midnight, $400 an hour after midnight. Evening rates include use of the Underwood and Reception Rooms and the grounds.

Other charges include a $100 membership fee, a $75 janitorial fee, and a $100 per hour catering fee after 10:00 P.M.

FACILITIES FOR THE PHYSICALLY HANDICAPPED?
YES NO SOME
          X

The first floor of the house is accessible to the handicapped.

How to Book Group Seating for Theater Performances

After a busy day of staging your own events, you and your associates might like nothing better than to sit back and watch a fine performance staged at one of Washington's wonderful theaters. Here are a few tips about how to book groups of seats for a performance.

Maybe you don't care whether your group sits together for a performance. Or maybe you do. Either way, according to staff at each theater, your best bet for reserving the number of seats you want is simply to call early, weeks ahead of time if possible, to make reservations. Even so, you may be out of luck; popular shows are often sold out way ahead of time. The procedure followed by area theaters for booking groups of seats is fairly standard. After you call to order tickets, the theater sends you a contract. You sign the contract and return it by the date and with the deposit amount stipulated in the document. Sometimes a theater requires immediate full payment to confirm reservations; sometimes it requires a 20 percent deposit.

Usually groups of 20 or more may qualify for a group discount. The amount you are discounted depends on any of a number of factors: what type of organization you are, how many tickets you want, the seats and performance day you're reserving, and the policy of the show's producer or promoter. Sometimes no discounts are available. The Kennedy Center, for example, never discounts tickets for Friday and Saturday night performances. If your group is eligible for a discounted price at any of the theaters, you can expect it to start at about 10 percent.

Many Washington area theaters have a special number to call if you want to book seats for a group. Here are a few:

Arena Stage: **202/554-9066**

Folger Shakespeare Theater: **202/547-3230**

Ford Theater: **202/638-2368**

Kennedy Center for the Performing Arts: **202/634-7201 (in Washington), *1-800/424-8504* (long-distance)**

National Theater: **1-800/233-3123**

The Source: **202/462-1073**

The Studio: 202/232-7267

Warner Theater: 202/626-1075

Wolf Trap: 703/225-1855

How to arrange special tours of the White House, and official briefings at the White House or on Capitol Hill

The first thing you want to do to arrange either a special tour of the White House, a briefing by White House officials or a briefing on Capitol Hill, is to call your company's or association's government relations office in Washington and ask them to handle the matter. The government relations office staff are people whose daily business it is to represent your organization's interests before Congress and the Executive Branch. This means that they usually are familiar with congressional and White House procedures.

If your organization doesn't have a Washington office to help you, here are some basic tips on what to do:

White House Special Tours

To arrange a special White House tour for your organization, you need to be in touch with the office of a senator or congressman with whom you have a constituency relationship. Ask for the staff person who handles special tours of the White House, explain what your organization is and request that a "group tour letter" be sent to the White House to obtain permission and tickets for the tour. The White House sends the tickets to the requesting member's office and the member's staff person then notifies you that your tickets have arrived. You can pick up the tickets on the Hill or at the member's district or state office, or have the tickets mailed to you.

Special White House tours are very popular—the White House fields over 535 requests daily—so you should try to make your arrangements at least a month in advance. Summer is nearly an impossible time to schedule a special White House viewing because of all the tourists visiting Washington with the same idea. The White House allots each congressman's and senator's office only ten tickets weekly, so the chances are that your group won't be allowed to exceed that number. The White House conducts four special tours each morning at 8:15 A.M. with 50 people in each group, which means that you'll probably be joined with other "special" viewers.

Briefings by White House Officials

Briefings by White House officials can be difficult to arrange. According to the White House's Office of Public Liaison, the procedure for scheduling briefings changes so often that any published procedure would quickly be out-of-date. That office recommends that you call the main number at the White House (202/456-1414) and ask to speak to the scheduling office of the administration official(s) with whom you'd like to meet. The switchboard will then put you in touch with the right office. Be prepared to explain what your organization is and the issues you'd like to discuss. You can expect to be asked to submit your request in writing.

Briefings on Capitol Hill

The way in which you arrange briefings on Capitol Hill depends on whom you want to meet with, how many people are involved and whether there's a particular issue you'd like to discuss. If there are just a few of you and you want to meet with one particular congressman or senator, you call that member's office and set up an appointment. If there are more than a few of you or if you want to meet with several congressional members, you again call the members' offices directly to arrange a meeting. You then work with one member's office to reserve a conference room on the Hill. (In all instances, you're much more likely to get the biggest turnout of members if you hold your event on the Hill.)

Finally, if your group wants to brief or be briefed by members on a particular topic, you call the congressional committee that has jurisdiction over that issue. Then you request that a briefing be arranged between your organization and committee members in a conference room on the Hill. For example, if the American Medical Association wished to inform congressional members about the AMA's concerns on the issue of Medicare, one of the committees the association would need to call would be the Committee on Health and Human Services.

If you don't know which committees handle your issue, call the office of the congressman or senator representing your area and ask. You can get the office numbers of congressional members and committees by calling the main number at the U.S. Capitol (202/224-3121).

If your aim is to acquaint as many members as possible with your views on an issue, your best bet is to arrange the briefing through the office of the member with whom you have a constituent relationship or with whom you share a common interest in the issue. If they are willing, those members can reserve a conference room and might also agree to send invitations to the House or Senate at large, asking them to attend the briefing.

Something else you should know is that there are some marvelous meeting sites on Capitol Hill. These sites can be reserved only when the event you're holding is considered a congressionally related activity, that is, one that is sponsored by a congressional member. Three popular spots are the Mike Mansfield Room in the U.S. Capitol Building, the Cannon Caucus Room in the Cannon House Office Building and the U.S. Botanic Gardens.

The Mike Mansfield Room is a paneled chamber that can accommodate 120 people seated in rows of chairs (theater-style), or 90 people seated around conference tables. The Cannon Caucus Room is huge and elaborate, furnished with chandeliers and red carpeting. This room can accommodate 350 people, seated, and 550 people, standing, for a meeting; 250 people seated for a banquet; and 450 people for a stand-up reception. The U.S. Botanic Gardens is perhaps the most popular site and accepts reservations six months in advance. This spot is used primarily for receptions, for which it can accommodate 480 people. The conservatory may be used as well for sit-down banquets, for which it can accommodate 160 people. Your event takes place in two large galleries that are usually decorated with palm trees or fuchsia plants, but you get the run of the building while you're here.

Ask congressional staff members for other meeting place recommendations.

Topical Cross Reference

Grand Halls

Historic Sites

Marvelous Mansions 100 Years Old or Less

Geographic Index

Capitol Hill

Midtown Washington

Dupont Circle

Leesburg

Maryland Countryside

Old Town Alexandria

Suburban Maryland

Suburban Virginia

Alphabetic Index

An (H) indicates sites with facilities for the handicapped.

About the Author

Elise Hartman Ford is a native of Baltimore, Maryland. She received her B.A. in English from Holy Cross College in Worcester, Massachusetts, and worked for several years as an in-house writer for such companies as MCI, in Washington, D.C., and TRW, in Redondo Beach, California. In 1985, Ford turned full time to freelance writing for magazines, newspapers and company in-house publications. She resides in Chevy Chase, Maryland, with her husband, Jim, and their daughter, Caitlin. UNIQUE MEETING PLACES IN GREATER WASHINGTON is her first book.

A NOTE TO MEETING AND PARTY PLANNERS

If you would like to order additional copies of UNIQUE MEETING PLACES, please use order form on following page. These other EPM books on Washington subjects make excellent references and/or presentation gifts:

WALKING TOURS OF OLD WASHINGTON AND ALEXANDRIA. $100,000 might buy you the original Paul Hogarth watercolors reproduced here in full color, but then you'd be missing the engaging text and the convenience of taking it all along as you step back into the distinguished heritage preserved in our Capital's finest old buildings. Usable art; exquisite gift. 8½ × 11. $24.95

FOOTNOTE WASHINGTON.   Bryson Rash, one of Washington's most beloved broadcasters, takes readers down the engaging, humorous and surprising bypaths of capital history. Inspired by President Truman's tale of a sex change on an equestrian statue, this is not the most important book ever to come out of Washington, but certainly the most entertaining. Illustrated. $8.95

THE WALKER WASHINGTON GUIDE.   The sixth edition of the "guide's guide to Washington," completely revised by Katharine Walker, builds on a 25-year reputation as the top general guide to the capital. Its 320 pages are packed with museums, galleries, hotels, restaurants, theaters, shops, churches, as well as sights. Beautiful maps and photos. Indispensable. $6.95

MR. LINCOLN'S CITY.   For any Civil War buff. Hidden among the impressive buildings and landscaped lawns of modern Washington are innumerable reminders of the heroic, tumultuous years 1861–1865. This engrossing guide to those historic sites doubles as illustrated history, with 130 photographs and 15 excellent maps. 8½ × 11. $14.95

GOING PLACES WITH CHILDREN IN WASHINGTON.   Still going strong after all these years; now in its 11th edition. Choose from more than 400 activities great for kids. Entries include information about hours, fees, tours, snack areas and restrooms. A must for parents, teachers and visiting families. $5.95

MILESTONES INTO HEADSTONES.   These mini biographies of 50 fascinating Americans buried in Washington are loaded with entertaining anecdotes. Find out why Abner Doubleday has been benched as baseball's inventor, how Peggy Eaton caused Andrew Jackson's entire cabinet to resign, and why John Philip Sousa became a tobacco pitchman. Forty photographs. $9.95

WASHINGTON COOKBOOK. If dinner conversation is going to turn to politics anyway, you might as well start the meal off with Nancy Reagan's Onion Wine Soup and finish with Bess Truman's Brownies. In between you can choose from among 500 other memorable recipes collected from Washington notables for the benefit of the Washington Opera. Illustrations. $10.00

OLD ALEXANDRIA. The most complete and authoritative guide to George Washington's hometown, offering walking tours as well as delightfully readable, carefully researched history of this old port. Along streets that retain their 18th century charm stand dozens of American architectural and cultural gems; OLD ALEXANDRIA takes you there. 65 photographs. $9.95

The form below can be used for orders of fewer than ten books. For quantity discounts, please write us or call 703-442-7810.

ORDER BLANK. Mail with check to:
EPM Publications, Box 490, McLean, VA 22101

Title	Qty	Price	Amount

Subtotal	_____
Virginia residents add 4½% tax	_____
Add $2 shpg. first book, $1 ea. add'l.	_____
Total	_____

Name _____

Street _____

City _____ State _____ Zip _____

Remember to enclose names, addresses and enclosure cards for gift purchases. Prices are subject to change. Write or call for free catalog: 703-442-7810.